Languages at work, competent multilinguals and the pedagogical challenges of COVID-19

Edited by Alessia Plutino and Elena Polisca

esearch-publishing.net

esearch-publishing.net

Published by Research-publishing.net, a not-for-profit association
Contact: info@research-publishing.net

Languages at work, competent multilinguals and the pedagogical challenges of COVID-19
Edited by Alessia Plutino and Elena Polisca

Publication date: 2021/02/26

Typeset by Research-publishing.net
Cover layout by © 2021 Raphaël Savina (raphael@savina.net)

ISBN13: 978-2-490057-83-2 (Ebook, PDF, colour)
ISBN13: 978-2-490057-84-9 (Ebook, EPUB, colour)
ISBN13: 978-2-490057-82-5 (Paperback - Print on demand, black and white)
Print on demand technology is a high-quality, innovative and ecological printing method; with which the book is never 'out of stock' or 'out of print'.

British Library Cataloguing-in-Publication Data.
A cataloguing record for this book is available from the British Library.

Legal deposit, France: Bibliothèque Nationale de France - Dépôt légal: février 2021.

Table of contents

Notes on contributors

Editors

Alessia Plutino is a FHEA and has worked as Senior Teaching Fellow of Italian at the University of Southampton and as an Associate Lecturer at the Open University for many years. Her career has focused on the teaching of Italian at undergraduate level (both F2F and online) as well as Italian, French, and German at secondary level. She has multiple research interests ranging from Computer Assisted Language Learning (CALL) and Telecollaboration to the use of micro blogging (Twitter), MOOCs, CoPs, and PLEs. She is now an independent educator and consultant and continues to work within both undergraduate and secondary sectors as a language ambassador and technology-for-languages enthusiast.

Elena Polisca is Senior Teaching Associate in Italian Studies at Lancaster University. Her academic interests include innovative approaches to language teaching and learning, development of digital language pedagogy, learner autonomy, digital language acquisition, language assessment, and digital feedback practices. She is also interested in nation-wide language educational policies. She teaches at all levels of the HE curriculum and directs the Progetto Lingua Italiana Dante Alighieri (PLIDA) examination centre at Lancaster.

Authors

Kate Borthwick is Principal Enterprise Fellow (Educational Innovation) in Modern Languages and Linguistics at the University of Southampton. She leads the University's MOOC programme as Director of Open Online Courses for the University and chairs the University Digital Education Working Group. She teaches and supervises postgraduate students in the area of technology-enhanced learning.

Stephan Caspar is a British/French educator and researcher currently living in Pittsburgh, Pennsylvania. His work at Carnegie Mellon University explores culture, language, and identity, with a focus on digital storytelling and immersive technologies. He brings experience in broadcast media, learning design, and education technology, with previous roles at the University of Southampton leading the Digital Learning Team and as a Content Producer at the BBC. You can follow Stephan on Twitter @dotsandspaces.

Prof. Sonia Cunico is Director of the Foreign Language Centre at the University of Exeter. She has taught Italian language and culture, translation studies, and linguistics in a number of UK HE Institutions for over 25 years. She has a wide experience as a teacher trainer and been involved in many national and international projects, such as the EU funded European Universities Tandem Project (EUniTa) and the European Union Development Fund (ESIF) project.

Dr Paul Feldman is Chief Executive of Jisc, the UK higher, further education and skills sectors' not-for-profit organisation for digital services and solutions. Before joining Jisc, Paul was an executive partner at Gartner UK. Paul has spent over 20 years in a number of financial service organisations, both in IT and business roles. Paul also worked in knowledge-based IT companies including Thomson Reuters Legal UK and the Intellectual Property Office.

Cecilia Goria is Associate Professor in the Department of Modern Languages and Cultures, University of Nottingham. She holds the role of Director of Digital Learning in the Faculty of Arts and is the Academic Leader of the distance learning Master's Degree in Digital Technologies for Language Teaching. Her research interests are concerned with the design, principles, and practice of open learning, active learning, participatory pedagogies in online, and blended teaching and learning.

Dale Munday is Digital Learning Facilitator at Lancaster University and PhD student in E-research and Technology Enhanced Learning. Dale has wide and varied experience in education, from teaching entry-level qualifications in prison education to Masters level in Higher Education institutions. He is a published author, with his chapter on inclusion and diversity in Post Compulsory Education and Training (PCET) being a career highlight. His recent work around shifting the expectations and capabilities of a VLE has led to an array of opportunities in consulting on digital education and curriculum design.

Dr Hélène Pulker is Senior Lecturer in French at the School of Languages and Applied Linguistics at the Open University, UK. She has extended experience in designing, writing, and implementing undergraduate courses for distance and online language learning. Her research focuses on the reuse of Open Educational Resources for online language teaching and online language teacher training. She is a member of the editorial board of the French Journal Distance and Mediation of Knowledge, and a reviewer for several other journals.

Fernando Rosell-Aguilar is Senior Teaching Fellow in Spanish at the School of Modern Languages and Cultures at the University of Warwick, United Kingdom. He also teaches Computer Assisted Language Learning (CALL) at Coventry University. Fernando is a Senior Fellow of the Higher Education Academy. He holds an MA in Online and Distance Learning from The Open University and has recently submitted his PhD Thesis. His research focuses on online language learning, mainly the use of apps, Twitter, and podcasting as teaching and learning tools. Other research interests include the use of multimodal synchronous online conferencing and task design.

Marion Sadoux is Head of Modern Language Programmes for the University of Oxford Language Centre which she joined in 2017. Marion has been teaching languages in Higher Education for over 30 years and is a keen language learner herself. Her areas of research are related to the link (or lack of?) between theories of second language acquisition and language teaching – particularly through technology-enhanced language learning.

Dr Ursula Stickler is Senior Lecturer in German at the School of Languages and Applied Linguistics at the Open University, UK. She has created German distance teaching materials for students from beginners' level to degree level. Her research expertise includes technology-enhanced language learning, professional development for language teachers in integrating Information and Communication Technology (ICT), the use of eye-tracking for researching synchronous online language learning environments, and qualitative research methods. She is co-editor of the book series 'Developing Online Language Pedagogies'.

Sascha Stollhans (@SaschaStollhans) is Senior Teaching Associate in German Studies at Lancaster University, where he also coordinates the German year abroad, the schools outreach programme for the Department of Languages and Cultures, and a global summer school. His academic interests include Germanic and Romance languages and linguistics, second language acquisition, digital approaches to teaching and learning, as well as educational policy. He currently co-leads the German strand of the national 'Linguistics in Modern Foreign Languages' project.

Dr Elodie Vialleton is Senior Lecturer in French at the School of Languages and Applied Linguistics at the Open University, UK. She has designed, authored, and taught distance French studies modules and courses for distance study at the Open University for over 15 years. Currently her main research focus is learning design and curriculum development in distance language teaching. She also researches the linguistic analysis of spoken French and English, and the teaching of listening and speaking skills, especially at a distance, and in particular the use of naturally-occurring speech in language teaching.

Gloria Visintini is Academic Educator with expertise and a passion for digital education. After teaching Italian at Bristol for years, in 2011 her role was extended to support colleagues across the Faculty of Arts to teach through innovative methods. In 2013 Gloria was awarded the University of Bristol Teaching Fellowship and in 2015 she won the Bristol Education Award. She became a Fellow of the UK Higher Education Academy in 2016.

Jocelyn Wyburd is Director of the Language Centre at the University of Cambridge, with a background in language teaching and advising. She is a former Chair of the University Council for Modern Languages in the UK, representing languages disciplines. She has led programmes promoting the study of languages and participated in national initiatives around language education strategies and policies. She regularly serves on strategic and quality reviews of university language centres and departments nationally and internationally.

Acknowledgements

This publication could not have been possible without the support, advice, coordination, and generosity of Research-publishing.net, who, as part of their *Give Back* campaign, have allowed us to publish this book. We wish to thank them publicly for their generosity and yet again another opportunity to support the wider language community to be heard, raise issues, and share experiences.

We are also very thankful to all the authors who have embraced our call and shared their expertise, knowledge, and views, and did so in such a collegial way during the challenging times of COVID-19.

Alessia Plutino and Elena Polisca

Introduction

Alessia Plutino[1] and Elena Polisca[2]

1.   Background

The title of this book, *Languages at work, competent multilinguals and the pedagogical challenges of COVID-19*, explores two issues that have become increasingly prominent in 2020. The first one reflects on the language skills which are in demand in the UK, where much-needed multilinguals are sought after in the job market. It challenges the link between employability and the global graduate concept, highlighting the need for language students to be able to sell their skills. The second issue, which resulted in the delayed publication of our book, focuses on COVID-19 and illustrates the challenge to which the education establishment stood up. It reports on practical examples of how educators and digital technologists reframed the whole teaching and learning context without compromising staff and students' experience.

The volume has, therefore, been deliberately conceived as two separate, yet interlinked, parts, showing explicitly how the editors felt the need, half-way through the process, to revisit their initial idea in the light of the unprecedented scenario which unfolded globally during the Spring of 2020.

The theme for the first part of the book draws inspiration from the All-Party Parliamentary Group (APPG) on Modern Languages' Manifesto, published in 2014 to tackle the "need for a national recovery programme"[3] and improve the

1. University of Southampton, Southampton, United Kingdom; plutinoalessia@gmail.com; https://orcid.org/0000-0001-5552-6753

2. Lancaster University, Lancaster, United Kingdom; e.polisca@lancaster.ac.uk

3. https://www.britishcouncil.org/education/schools/support-for-languages/thought-leadership/appg/news/manifesto-for-languages

How to cite: Plutino, A., & Polisca, E. (2021). Introduction. In A. Plutino & E. Polisca (Eds), *Languages at work, competent multilinguals and the pedagogical challenges of COVID-19* (pp. 1-7). Research-publishing.net. https://doi.org/10.14705/rpnet.2021.49.1213

nation's linguistic skills base. Subsequently, in March 2019 a further call for action from APPG was released stating that 'the UK is in a language crisis'. Whilst employers are increasingly seeking multilinguals whose language skills are valued as an asset within the job market, UK educational settings are witnessing a consistent decline of language learners across sectors, creating a deficiency in the workforce and a shift towards monolingualism.

The current political and economic uncertainty is also contributing to widening the gap between offer and demand of multilinguals, with European schemes to support student mobility being under threat. It is within the context outlined above that the articles in this first part of the book explore and support the concept of the global language graduate. In particular, the focus is placed on the need for students to learn how to understand and articulate what makes them stand out from the crowd, as well as the need to be able to showcase the valuable, transferable skills that can be gained through studying languages.

2.   Part 1

The book opens with a reference to the timely *Policy Briefing on Languages, Business, Trade and Innovation* published in June 2020, by Wendy Ayres-Bennett and Janice Carruther, which "focuses on the importance of languages for business, trade, and innovation" (p. 3). The briefing reports on the scale of how language skills deficit is currently affecting UK business and trade as well as "leading to an overdependence on anglophone export markets" (Ayres-Bennett & Carruthers, 2020, p. 3). It represents yet another strong call for the need of more language skills and cultural fluency which can only be achieved by a coherent and consistent language policy across the UK education sector. A competence in languages also brings a whole range of soft skills which are highly sought after by employers highlighting the fact that language graduates should not simply be seen as 'linguists'. This point is strongly supported in the article by **Jocelyn Wyburd**, *'Linguist' or 'Global Graduate'? A matter of identity for the global graduate with language skills*. Here, the author discusses the importance for graduate students to be able to articulate the whole range of transferable competencies that they develop during their degree in a cogent manner. The author makes a lucidly convincing argument about the importance of language and intercultural skills for employability, touching also on English *lingua franca* and Brexit. She discusses and challenges the issue of language graduates who identify themselves simply as 'linguists' and provides a framework for students – supported by educators – which can be used to translate graduates' skillset and experiences into the language used by employers.

In the next contribution, a team of researchers and practitioners from the Open University, **Hélène Pulker, Ursula Stickler, and Elodie Vialleton**, continues to highlight the link between language skills and employability by reporting on a radically redesigned modern languages curriculum in The School of Languages and Applied Linguistics; which eventually led to the development of a new Employability Framework. The article focuses on redefining modern languages as a holistic cluster of knowledge, skills, and attributes where it is important to develop a pedagogic approach which encourages self-reflection and explicit training in articulating one's skills as a 'well-rounded, global graduate'.

The first part of the book comprises fewer articles than originally planned; several authors who had agreed to write on the theme of language graduates and employability were sadly affected, one way or another, by the first wave of the pandemic. With COVID-19 taking hold of, and bringing, 2020 to a standstill, as editors of this publication we felt the need to expand our original call for papers to include a snapshot of how the spread of the virus started to impact the educational sector. In particular, our focus was readjusted to include the way in which the pandemic started to redefine teaching and learning and, more loosely, the development of the skills of language graduates.

3.　Part 2

Following the rapid spread of the virus, schools, colleges, and universities in the UK and across the world had to switch from face-to-face to online teaching almost overnight. It was evident from the start that the whole teaching community across the sector was reacting to the challenges brought into education by the pandemic both with concerns and renewed energy. To provide a flavour of this exceptionally fast-paced pedagogical shift, we asked selected colleagues covering various roles within the higher education sector to write a reflective piece on their experience of researching, teaching, designing, and training staff during the first wave of the pandemic for the benefit of the entire language community. The second part of our publication offers readers the opportunity to consider, and reflect on, the changes affecting their individual practices with a wider focus on language learning and language graduates' attributes.

Articles from this second call are featured in the second part of this publication. They are of a more personal and reflective nature, providing an overview of how the pandemic has accelerated the transition into a new modality which had already been predicted, but whose practical realisation was pushed forward at speed.

This section opens with **Paul Feldman**, Jisc CEO, reflecting on how the effort to make the most of an unforeseen and challenging situation like COVID-19 brought the future of learning forward. He suggests the adoption by the whole sector of an innovative approach that *firmly* integrates face-to-face with virtual interaction. He sees the forced acceleration in online teaching and assessment practices as a sustainable model for the post-COVID world of education.

The theme is then taken forward by three articles looking at how Digital Learning colleagues in Higher Education (HE) institutions worked on the 'transposing' of face-to-face teaching to online. Difficulties posed by the online modality for teaching and assessment are also discussed, with some suggestions for the future. In reporting on the initial steps taken in her own institution to respond to the COVID-19 emergency measures, **Cecilia Goria** explores the myth of academics not favouring digital pedagogies. She reflects on the process of moving forward from the state of emergency to a more thought-through digital pedagogical approach where academics embrace digital pedagogies as a meaningful part of their practice.

A personal perspective is offered by **Gloria Visintini**, who describes the practice of her institution during the pandemic. She reflects, in her role as Director of Digital Learning in the School of Modern Languages at Bristol University, on how the digital education agenda was brought forward by COVID-19 and how having a background in language teaching helped, and informed, some of her conversations with teaching staff. She describes the educational guidelines that were put in place and implemented by colleagues in Modern Languages and discusses the new digital teaching and assessment practices, the challenges in delivering teaching, and the opportunities the new online landscape created for staff and students.

Dale Munday's article offers a report on how his institution supported its staff in the rapid shift to online teaching and learning, with an approach centred around the upskilling of staff. The future of curriculum design and the associated requirements at an institutional- and sector-wide level is also addressed in relation to the opportunities and challenges faced.

Linked to the topic of staff upskilling in a wider context, **Fernando Rosell-Aguilar**'s article looks at his own experience as a Twitter user and online pedagogy expert to reflect on how the use of Twitter during the pandemic reinforced the sharing of good practice among education professionals by providing a source of advice, ideas, and resources in a collegial way.

Kate Borthwick offers an overview of the practicalities of moving the Pre-sessional programme at the University of Southampton, a study skills and English language programme designed to prepare international students for academic success in UK Higher Education, to online delivery. She discusses how this was achieved using Blackboard, MS Teams, and Padlet, and how a personalised, small-group teaching experience was re-created.

The way the Modern Languages team at the University of Oxford saw the switch of their language courses to a remote mode as an opportunity to develop new ways of designing and delivering language courses is explored by **Marion Sadoux**. Her article also discusses a flexible and hybrid future of language teaching.

The book then moves on to explore another important asset in terms of the employability skills of graduate language courses: the year abroad. This compulsory practice of graduates spending the third year of their degree abroad was enormously affected by the sudden closure of many countries' borders and ban to travel during the first wave of the pandemic as institutions had to respond with fast and practical solutions, which would not compromise degree outcomes for language graduates.

Sonia Cunico looks at the impact that the pandemic had on the year abroad. In her creative contribution based on the metaphor of journey, she describes how Exeter University students were offered alternative online language provision to support their learning once their year abroad was cut short due to COVID-19.

Sascha Stollhans is also reflecting on how unprecedented circumstances affected the year abroad as well as exploring the delivery of teaching and learning activities in higher education, including assessment. He offers a positive view for the future of the sector and recognises the spirit of collegiality developed during the pandemic across different HE institutions and national organisations.

The book closes with the contribution of **Stephan Caspar**, a UK practitioner currently teaching in the USA. In his piece, he reflects on essential skills that language graduates develop with language learning and multicultural studies. It is a very personal account on how, during the pandemic, he managed to help students find their voice and become active agents of change through storytelling. He highlights the potential of this methodology to help communities draw parallels with, and face, wider issues concerning minorities within a challenged society. American education has been profoundly shaken both by COVID-19 and the Black Lives Matter movement; both reiterated the importance of language learning, cultural understanding, and identity as useful employability skills for the new global graduates to support, rebuild, and unite communities, especially in challenging times.

We hope that this volume will inspire practitioners to find ways to help raise language graduates' awareness about the real value of their degree and the range of skills that come with it. Most importantly, we hope that the volume will reinforce the concept of the global graduate as one that cannot be separated from language learning, cultural awareness, and multiculturalism. Throughout the book, the pursuit of a common objective should emerge: the language sector can bring a solid contribution to the tackling of contemporary crises – both at a national and local level.

By adding the second part devoted to personal reflections on education in a worldwide pandemic, we hope to leave a tangible sign of how educators rose to the challenge and found the strength to overcome the emergency and accelerate innovative approaches which had already emerged in the education scenario but have otherwise taken a longer time.

Reference

Ayres-Bennett, W., & Carruthers, J. (2020). *Policy briefing on languages, business, trade and innovation*. AHRC. https://www.modernlanguagesleadershipfellow.com/app/uploads/2020/07/POLICY-BRIEFING.-LANGUAGES-BUSINESS-TRADE-AND-INNOVATION.pdf

Part 1.

1 'Linguist' or 'Global Graduate'? A matter of identity for the global graduate with language skills

Jocelyn Wyburd[1]

Abstract

In this chapter, I examine the problematic issue of identifying as a 'linguist' for graduates who have studied languages, in an employability context. I challenge them to reframe their identity as 'global graduates', with reference to the competencies outlined in the *Global Graduates into Global Leaders* report (NCUB, 2011). In the process, I also demonstrate why a truly global graduate needs also to be a linguist, in spite of the hegemony of English as a global *lingua franca,* and in the context of Brexit. I provide a framework for use by students, with support from educators, to translate their skill sets and experiences into the language of employers. I hope that this will provide a clear guide to the importance not just of developing, but also articulating cogently a range of competencies which are transferable to the global economy and global society, and a convincing argument for the importance of language and intercultural skills within that portfolio.

Keywords: global graduate, global competencies, English lingua franca, Brexit.

A graduating linguist at a careers fair asks, "what jobs do you have for linguists?"; the answer is "none, we outsource our translation requirements". Similarly, a student seeking graduate roles which explicitly ask for languages might be disappointed by the lack of choice and range available. These

1. University of Cambridge, Cambridge, United Kingdom; jmw234@cam.ac.uk

How to cite: Wyburd, J. (2021). 'Linguist' or 'Global Graduate'? A matter of identity for the global graduate with language skills. In A. Plutino & E. Polisca (Eds), *Languages at work, competent multilinguals and the pedagogical challenges of COVID-19* (pp. 11-21). Research-publishing.net. https://doi.org/10.14705/rpnet.2021.49.1214

scenarios can challenge university linguists – students of languages and those who have learnt languages alongside degrees in other subjects – to question their study choices when considering graduate employment. Such scenarios also pose a challenge for (particularly UK) university staff who promote language study in order to break the mould of Anglophone monolingualism, and for global citizenship and employability in a global economy. Studying languages is much more than the acquisition of an instrumental transactional skill, but do students and employers alike sufficiently recognise this? Do educators need to find a new 'language' to help students identify the wider employability attributes they have gained in the process? I will explore what that new 'language' needs to be comprised of, while not neglecting the intrinsic value of language skills themselves.

University students will often self-identify according to their (main) subject of study: *I'm an engineer, a physicist, a historian, a lawyer, a linguist, a medic*, etc. In some disciplines, this terminology transfers directly into a professional identity, usually refined by further training: e.g. as an engineer or lawyer. Similarly, professional linguists – language teachers and academics, translators, and interpreters – become so through specialist postgraduate training. The subject-oriented identity is left behind by most graduates when they progress from being a social scientist, zoologist, philosopher, or linguist to employment, which is then accompanied by a new professional title. Few history graduates who go into banking or the civil service will continue to identify primarily as historians – and this applies equally to linguists. As graduates cease to be students and become something else with a new identity, they undergo multiple transitions requiring a considerable amount of adaptation and the adoption of new terminology.

The British Academy's (2016) *Born Global* research observed that languages graduates were, compared to their peers, "often less capable of articulating the knowledge, skills, and attributes that they have acquired through their degree courses, and how these may be relevant to future employers" (p. 13). It is therefore incumbent on university educators of linguists to facilitate their students' learning of yet another 'language' to address this deficit.

In an age of globalisation, the concept of the 'global graduate' is particularly pertinent. Drawing on evidence from business and graduate recruiters, the *Global Graduates into Global Leaders* report includes a ranked list of 14 'global competencies' (NCUB, 2011, p. 8). Multilingualism is at number 11, but this should not dishearten linguists, as, higher up, we find *an ability to embrace multiple perspectives and challenge thinking* and *an openness to and respect for a range of perspectives from around the world*. Several others incorporate cross-cultural and multi-cultural dimensions, as well as *multi-cultural learning agility*. These competencies are summarised in a framework (NCUB, 2011, p. 12) under three interrelated headings of *cultural agility*, *global mindset*, and *relationship management* underpinned by the core competencies of *learning agility* and *adaptability*. Each has more specific overarching competencies, such as *resilience, multilingualism, multi-cultural knowledge, social etiquette, negotiating, influencing and leading teams,* and *empathy.*

The NCUB's (2011) framework corresponds felicitously to the *Born Global* assertion that

> "the attributes of languages graduates go beyond technical linguistic skills, important though those undoubtedly are, and even beyond intercultural understanding, embracing analytical rigour, resilience, the ability to communicate sensitively and subtly and the maturity and independence which come from studying or working abroad" (The British Academy, 2016, p. 12).

I have therefore used the NCUB (2011) global graduate framework as the basis of a toolkit I propose to promote critical thinking and reflection on student development through language and related studies and experiences.

Any student can map their formal and informal learning and developmental experiences onto this framework and, thus, articulate their identity as a global graduate. In Table 1 below, I suggest how university linguists might do so. Students may need support from educators in the process of developing their new identity and in engaging with the critical reflection required to evidence it.

This also builds on my previous related work (Wyburd, 2017) looking at how the terminology of the Quality Assurance Agency (QAA) subject benchmark statement for languages, cultures, and societies (QAA, 2019[2]) can be used to articulate employability competencies.

Table 1.   Mapping graduates in and with languages onto the Global Graduate (NCUB, 2011) skill set

Skill set	Sub-skill	Can be developed through...
Cultural Agility	Resilience	• Residence abroad
		• Coping with challenges (studies, personal life)
		• Working/studying/living with people of different cultures (at home/abroad)
		• Navigating different ways of thinking and living
	Multi-lingualism	• Language degrees
		• Language learning alongside other studies
		• Language acquisition while abroad
		• Active use of heritage language(s)/ bilingual background
		• Reflecting on/contrasting different ways of communicating
Global Mindset	Multi-cultural knowledge	• Studying literature/culture/history/philosophy/ politics/society/religions/economics, etc. from wider perspectives (breaking away from Anglocentric 'norms')
		• Contrasting perspectives from different cultural traditions
		• (Multi-) cultural learning from residence abroad
	Social etiquette	• Sensitivity to contrastive norms of behaviour – willingness to adapt
		• Studying communication styles
		• Studying contrastive rhetorical traditions – discourse analysis in L1s and L2s
		• Critically observing behavioural norms when abroad/in multi-cultural contexts
		• Online etiquette in multi-cultural communications

---

2. The 2015 version was referenced in that chapter, but it has now been replaced by an updated version, which is materially still entirely relevant to the argument made.

Cultural Agility and Global Mindset	Empathy	• Living/working/studying alongside others from diverse backgrounds: (1) building awareness of other perspectives/views and (2) building rapport and respect for diversity/otherness
Relationship Management	Negotiating and influencing	• Communication skills – from project work, language classes, other
		• Group projects – team-work at university/work experience
		• Student societies/sports
		• Multi-cultural multi-lingual teams/groups (at home/during residence abroad)
		• Navigating online learning and social spaces
	Leading teams	• Work experience
		• Student societies/sports
		• For further development in employment – aspirational for new graduates
Core skills underpinning all the above	Learner agility	• Learning new skills, e.g. language learning alongside other subjects
		• Learning in unfamiliar contexts – abroad, work experience
		• Learning in multi-cultural groups/ through L2 medium
		• Developing new skills and behaviours in response to diverse contexts (including online/remote learning)
	Adaptability	• Residence abroad – adapting to new lifestyle, environment, culture
		• Working/studying with people from different backgrounds/cultures – abroad or at home
		• Responding to cultural and contextual challenges (including online/remote learning and cross-cultural social interaction)

The majority of the global graduate competencies are commonly described as 'soft skills' – personal attributes which enable human interaction. These can be seen (unhelpfully) as being of lower value than the 'harder' technical or scientific skills of relevance to specific industries, which are largely by-products of STEM subjects. In an attempt to redress this imbalance, The British Academy (2017) published *The right skills*, celebrating the skills developed by Arts, Humanities, and Social Sciences (AHSS) graduates and their contributions to the global economy in a wide range of sectors. They followed it in 2020 with *Qualified for the future* (The British Academy, 2020) to provide quantitative evidence of the tangible benefits of those skills to the UK workforce, economy, and society, now and for the future.

In these publications, AHSS graduates are described as acquiring high-level skills, crucial in a data-and digital-driven environment and a global context, particularly noting increasing demand for *adaptability* and *flexibility* in a fast-changing world. They classify the core AHSS graduate skills under three broad headings: (1) *communication and collaboration*, (2) *research and analysis*, and (3) *attitudes and behaviours characterised by independence and adaptability*, while noting additional subject-specific skills, such as languages. It is important that student linguists recognise that they are likely to have broadly the same skill sets as other AHSS graduates, but with the crucial addition of languages and the by-products of residence abroad experiences enhanced by their language skills. Thus, the graduate linguist needs also to redefine their identity, not so much as a linguist but as an AHSS graduate with additional highly valuable benefits.

In 2020, during the global COVID-19 pandemic, the use of online video communications has forced everyone to refine their communication skills, with less reliance on body language and other non-verbal clues. When communicating in a second language and cross-culturally, the challenge presented is even greater. As a result, university linguists should be even better equipped for a future global work and trading model which may increasingly rely on remote communication.

Multilingualism itself could, from both the NCUB (2011) and The British Academy (2016, 2017, 2019, 2020) reports, be seen as a valuable addition, rather than crucial to the 21st century global graduate. It is therefore worth exploring two factors which may be erroneously contributing to the side-lining of language skills in this context. One of these is the prevalence of English as a global *lingua franca*. The other is Brexit. I consider each in turn below.

In Anglophone countries, campaigners for language learning have for decades attempted to counteract the perception that the rest of the world speaks English, obviating the need for other languages. In 2002, the Barcelona European Council adopted an aspiration for EU citizens of proficiency in the mother tongue plus two languages, recommending the systematic teaching of two languages in statutory education. In 2016, an average of 94% of pupils (excluding UK students) in upper secondary education were studying English, while the next most studied language was Spanish (21.5%) and 59.4% were studying two or more languages (Eurostat, 2018). In the UK, however, since 2002, language learning has declined dramatically in secondary schools, and only 46% of 16 year olds in England took a General Certificate of Secondary Education (GCSE) qualification in any foreign language in 2018, as reported by the BBC (Jeffreys, 2019).

Does the hegemony of English as a Lingua Franca (ELF) threaten the learning of languages other than English, whether in the UK or elsewhere? Smokotin, Alekseyenko, and Petrova (2014) observed that ELF "falls under the influence of the speaker's native language and culture both at the phonetic and lexical-grammatical levels" and that "ELF speakers need not follow strictly linguistic and cultural norms of the English language native speakers since ELF communication frequently occurs without their participation" (p. 511). They point out that, where English was learnt traditionally as a foreign language, closely associated with the national cultures of major English-speaking nations, ELF is now a vehicle for communication between numerous different cultures, with English-speaking nations not necessarily represented. These observations represent a challenge to native English speakers who may pepper their language with culturally rich references and idioms, and/or fail to adapt phonetically or lexico-grammatically to the ELF environment they find themselves in.

The ELF medium itself is, thus, both culturally neutral and simultaneously a vehicle for highly diverse forms of cultural expression and identity which risk being mutually misunderstood. Hülmbauer, Böhringer, and Seidlhofer (2008) observed that in an ELF context, "as far as intercultural competences and strategies are concerned, native speakers are frequently disadvantaged due to their lack of practice in these processes and over-reliance on English as their L1" (p. 27).

Jenkins (2018) similarly observes that

> "[t]ranscultural communication skills are therefore paramount [and that] more successful ELF communicators will be able to adjust (or accommodate) their own use of English or other languages (so as to make it more appropriate for their interlocutors), and their own receptive expectation (so as to more easily understand what is being said to them)" (p. 26).

Crucially, the author asserts that

> "the process of having learnt another language or languages is helpful in being understood by alerting speakers to what kinds of linguistic features non-native speakers may find difficult to understand in English [and that] many native English speakers lack both these skill sets" (p. 26).

In the same chapter, she cites an example from Van Parijs (2011) of EU meetings in which speakers of diverse nationalities speak in English, with few, if any, listening to interpreters. But, "when a British or Irish participant takes the floor, you can often notice that some participants suddenly grab their earphones and start fiddling with the channel selector" (Jenkins, 2018, p. 27).

The global graduate competencies considered above focused more on cross-cultural communication skills than on multilingualism per se. And yet, as seen here, multilingualism is actually crucial to cross-cultural ELF communication. Indeed, Jenkins (2018) reconceptualises ELF as being, by definition, a 'multilingua franca'; she goes on to warn that "those who are monolingual will increasingly find themselves left behind in supposedly 'English' interactions in which their conversation partners translanguage in and out of other languages" (pp. 28-31). From ELF studies, one can therefore infer that a truly global graduate must be multi-lingual.

Each year since the UK voted to leave the EU in June 2016, annual surveys of UK schools have noted a resultant negative influence on attitudes to language learning. *Language trends* 2019 reports that a significant minority of secondary schools cite Brexit as a "major challenge to the delivery of language teaching" (British Council, 2019, p. 15). Some respondents reported perceptions that leaving the EU actually *invalidates* the need for language learning, while others reported the opposite, noting stark differences in attitude depending on the socio-economic catchment area of specific schools and the multi-cultural make-up of the pupil cohort. The negative 'Brexit effect' on language learning may be short-lived once the reality of global trade and relationships, including with the remaining 27 EU members, drives ever greater need for languages.

Indeed, the *Languages after Brexit* collection of essays (Kelly, 2018) challenges the UK at all levels – individual, education, government – to take action on developing the language and intercultural skills the UK will need to thrive. In parallel, *Languages for the future* (British Council, 2017) explores the need for languages in the context of the UK's future place in the world post Brexit and its likely trading partners. In ranking world languages by importance, the report partly considers whether future relationships will be limited by the extent to which other countries are willing and able to use English as a medium of communication.

The challenges thrown down by both these publications are taken up in the *Call for action* published, remarkably, by all four national UK academies – for Arts, Humanities and Social Sciences, Science, Medicine, and Engineering (The British Academy, 2019) – which asserts that, if the UK became the 'linguistic powerhouse' it has the potential to be, it would be "more prosperous, productive, influential, innovative, knowledgeable, culturally richer, more socially cohesive, and, quite literally, healthier" (p. 2). It is very important that university students of all disciplines, including sciences, engineering, and medicine, recognise that, whatever the post-brexit trading model, languages will be fundamental to the global graduate skill set they will need to acquire. The importance of languages, and thus multi-lingual graduates to 'Global Britain' post Brexit, is further strengthened in the case studies from a range of economic and industrial sectors included in the 2020 MEITS/AHRC[3] policy briefing (Ayres-Bennett & Carruthers, 2020).

In conclusion, I have sought to demonstrate that the university linguist, whether a graduate of, or with, languages, needs to identify, in the context of employability, as a global graduate; and, furthermore, that a global graduate needs to be multi-lingual, in spite of the hegemony of ELF. I have sought to map the NCUB's (2011) global competencies, as 'high-level' skills, onto the opportunities that graduates of, and with, languages can develop through their university careers, including through residence abroad. Being a global graduate does not mean negating one's identity as a linguist, but is, instead, a translation of all that being a linguist comprises into a language which employers can relate to. Finally, I have sought to demonstrate that Brexit, far from invalidating the need for languages, will actually require greater multi-lingual capacity for the UK to thrive. University linguists are well placed to be truly global graduates because of their language skills and international experience. But, they will need to redefine themselves as such, rather than relying solely only on their identity as 'linguists'.

References

Ayres-Bennett, W., & Carruthers, J. (2020). *Policy briefing on languages, business, trade and innovation.* MEITS/AHRC. http://www.meits.org/publications/policy-documents

British Council. (2017). *Languages for the future: the foreign languages the United Kingdom needs to become a truly global nation.* British Council. Retrieved from: https://www.britishcouncil.org/sites/default/files/languages_for_the_future_2017.pdf

British Council. (2019). *Language Trends 2019 Language Teaching In Primary And Secondary Schools In England.* https://www.britishcouncil.org/sites/default/files/language-trends-2019.pdf

Eurostat. (2018). *Foreign language learning statistics.* https://ec.europa.eu/eurostat/statistics-explained/index.php?title=Foreign_language_learning_statistics#Upper_secondary_education

---

3. Multilingualism, Empowering Individuals and Transforming Societies (MEITS) project funded by the Arts & Humanities Research Council (AHRC).

Hülmbauer, C., Böhringer, H., & Seidlhofer, B. (2008). Introducing English as a lingua franca (ELF): precursor and partner in intercultural communication. *Synergies Europe, 3*, 25-36.

Jeffreys, B. (2019). *Language learning: German and French drop by half in UK schools.* BBC. https://www.bbc.co.uk/news/education-47334374

Jenkins, J. (2018). Trouble with English? In M. Kelly (Ed.), *Languages after Brexit: how the UK speaks to the world* (pp. 25-34). Palgrave Macmillan.

Kelly, M. (2018). (Ed.). *Languages after Brexit: how the UK speaks to the world.* Palgrave Macmillan.

NCUB. (2011). *Global graduates into global leaders.* National Centre for Universities and Business http://www.ncub.co.uk/reports/global-graduates-into-global-leaders.html

QAA. (2019). Subject benchmark statement: languages, cultures and societies. Quality Assurance Agency. https://www.qaa.ac.uk/docs/qaa/subject-benchmark-statements/subject-benchmark-statement-languages-cultures-and-societies.pdf

Smokotin, V. M., Alekseyenko, A. S., & Petrova, G. I. (2014). The phenomenon of linguistic globalization: English as the global lingua franca (EGLF). *Procedia - Social and Behavioral Sciences, 54*, 509-513. https://doi.org/10.1016/j.sbspro.2014.10.177

The British Academy. (2016). *Born global. Implications for higher education.* https://www.thebritishacademy.ac.uk/sites/default/files/Born%20Global%20-%20Implications%20 for%20Higher%20Education_1.pdf

The British Academy. (2017). *The right skills: celebrating skills in the arts, humanities and social sciences.* https://www.thebritishacademy.ac.uk/publications/right-skills-celebrating-skills-arts-humanities-and-social-sciences-ahss

The British Academy. (2019). *Languages in the UK: a call for action.* https://www.thebritishacademy.ac.uk/sites/default/files/Languages-UK-2019-academies-statement.pdf

The British Academy. (2020). *Qualified for the future: quantifying demand for arts, humanities and social sciences skills.* https://www.thebritishacademy.ac.uk/publications/skills-qualified-future-quantifying-demand-arts-humanities-social-science/

Van Parijs, S. (2011). *Linguistic justice for Europe and for the world.* Oxford University Press.

Wyburd, J. (2017). Transnational graduates and employability: challenges for HE languages departments. In C. Alvarez-Mayo, A. Gallagher Brett & F. Michel (Eds), *Innovative language teaching and learning at university: enhancing employability* (pp. 11-19). Research-publishing.net. https://doi.org/10.14705/rpnet.2017.innoconf2016.650

2 Well-rounded graduates – what languages can do

Hélène Pulker[1], Ursula Stickler[2], and Elodie Vialleton[3]

Abstract

The School of Languages and Applied Linguistics at the Open University (OU) radically re-designed its modern languages curriculum in 2014, launching its first suite of new modules in 2017. The institution as a whole has since also developed a new employability framework. Our paper describes the principles underpinning the design of the new curriculum, demonstrates how it is being implemented, and focuses on an initiative that involved our Associate Lecturers (ALs) in defining a 'well-rounded graduate' and reflecting on plurilingualism and their roles as language teachers in a distance-teaching institution. Presenting our Teaching Excellence project, its processes, and findings in this paper will allow colleagues who teach modern languages to replicate or adapt parts of our approach in their own settings, exemplifying to the wider world how language skills can become an inherent element of the well-rounded graduate in the 21st century.

Keywords: language graduates, employability, action research.

1. The Open University, Milton Keynes, United Kingdom; helene.pulker@open.ac.uk; https://orcid.org/0000-0003-0487-2642

2. The Open University, Milton Keynes, United Kingdom; ursula.stickler@open.ac.uk; https://orcid.org/0000-0002-8754-7134

3. The Open University, Milton Keynes, United Kingdom; elodie.vialleton@open.ac.uk; https://orcid.org/0000-0002-9944-7245

How to cite: Pulker, H., Stickler, U., & Vialleton, E. (2021). Well-rounded graduates – what languages can do. In A. Plutino & E. Polisca (Eds), *Languages at work, competent multilinguals and the pedagogical challenges of COVID-19* (pp. 23-35). Research-publishing.net. https://doi.org/10.14705/rpnet.2021.49.1215

1. Introduction

Globally and within Europe, the call for language competences as part of employability skills has become heard widely. Some Higher Education Institutions (HEIs) have already responded by integrating language and employability more closely. However, there is evidence that languages graduates are not necessarily aware of the range of employability skills they develop through their course, or are unable to articulate them. Moreover, practitioners on the ground might fear that the latter comes with a loss of language competence, and, hence, they might resist the change required in pedagogy to support it. Language teachers at tertiary level but also, consequently, at secondary and even primary level, will need to be encouraged to buy into the new curriculum and its associated methods and content.

The School of Languages and Applied Linguistics at the OU has revised their modern languages syllabus and curriculum considerably, following university strategic new priorities and responding to a changing higher education environment.

As a distance university, the OU differs from other HEIs in which all teachers have immediate and direct contact with students. In our case, the bulk of the academic teaching is done through materials design and development, and mediated through ALs to teach and support students. New requirements for graduateness demand a shift towards general communication and employability skills, amongst others, and this is reflected increasingly in our materials. However, although these changes have taken place centrally, they have not necessarily been transmitted effectively to all our ALs.

The Teaching Excellence project presented in this paper is aimed at re-connecting language ALs to our updated strategy for language teaching and materials design, and at cascading its rationale to other ALs. In addition, it is intended to gain immediate feedback and evaluation of the impact on students and teachers during language tutorials.

2.   The new curriculum and the principles underpinning its design

Research (e.g. Araújo et al., 2015) shows that knowledge of languages increases employability. For Kelly (2016), "[t]he value of languages for employment is not the only motivation for learning other languages, but language learning provides a lasting asset for a growing number of careers" (p. xix). In the UK, it has been recognised that languages are "strategically vital for the future of the UK" (The British Academy, 2020, p. 6). The positive impact of multilingualism on social cohesion has also been emphasised in a report from AHRC and UKRI (2019). The economic impact of the nation's lack of language skills has been costed at 3.5% of GDP (The British Academy, 2019). At the same time, the current higher education environment has seen languages departments having to justify or fight for their existence (too many of them unsuccessfully), and needing to demonstrate to their own institutions the value of their programmes and their relevance in a context where, more often than not, the focus is on the vocational relevance or monetary value of degrees for graduates. Employers do recognise that graduates with language skills add value to businesses through the range of skills developed as languages students, e.g. their communication skills or ability to work with people from diverse cultural backgrounds: "[f]or the government vision of 'Global Britain' to be delivered, businesses need people who can communicate with customers and suppliers around the world" (CBI/Pearson, 2019, p. 26). Languages specialists know that the development of such attributes is intrinsic to languages programmes, but they have, so far, frequently remained in the background, and been taught implicitly. As a consequence, awareness of these attributes has remained low in the general public and amongst non-specialists, and languages graduates themselves are often unable to articulate them, for example, in a job interview.

It has been shown that interventions can be successful in teaching students how to articulate their employability skills (Tomasson Goodwin, Goh, Verkoeyen, & Lithgow, 2019), and this is an integral part of the approach taken by the School of Languages and Applied Linguistics at the OU. Starting in 2013, we undertook a thorough review of the content of our modern languages curriculum (described in Baumann & Vialleton, 2017) in order to:

- foreground the development of all the skills, knowledge and attributes taught through a modern languages degree programme;

- raise awareness of the development of skills and of their relevance in terms of employability and in terms of other learning gains, working gains, and personal gains relevant to part-time adult learners reflecting the "holistic fusion of skills, values, and attitudes in [their] employment journeys" (Kellett & Clifton, 2017, n.p.); and

- help students to articulate this.

In the past, the development of OU modern languages modules hinged on three subject-specific areas, namely language skills, cultural knowledge, and language learning skills, which was reflected, for example, in the labelling of different content sections in our module materials. The new curriculum blueprint developed in our school follows a different design, which reflects a more holistic view of what language learning is about. It explicitly redefined the discipline as a clustering of knowledge, skills, competences, and attitudes spanning several different areas. Some of these are subject-specific, such as the development of grammatical competence or of intercultural communication skills, and others are not subject-specific, for example, digital skills and academic skills. In total, 12 core components where identified, around which the new curriculum blueprint was structured. This is illustrated in Figure 1 below (The Open University, 2017a).

Through this work, we redefined our languages graduates as well-rounded graduates able to demonstrate a wide range of skills, knowledge, and attitudes relevant to a variety of jobs and life situations. The impact on the overall content of the new modules produced since we started implementing the new curriculum blueprint was not dramatic, although it has had to be adapted to suit the revised framework; greater emphasis has also been put on intercultural communication competence. At the same time, a more substantial rethink of the way the course is framed, and of the narrative which introduces it to our students within the learning materials that we produce for them, had to be introduced.

Figure 1. The 12 components of the OU modern languages curriculum blueprint

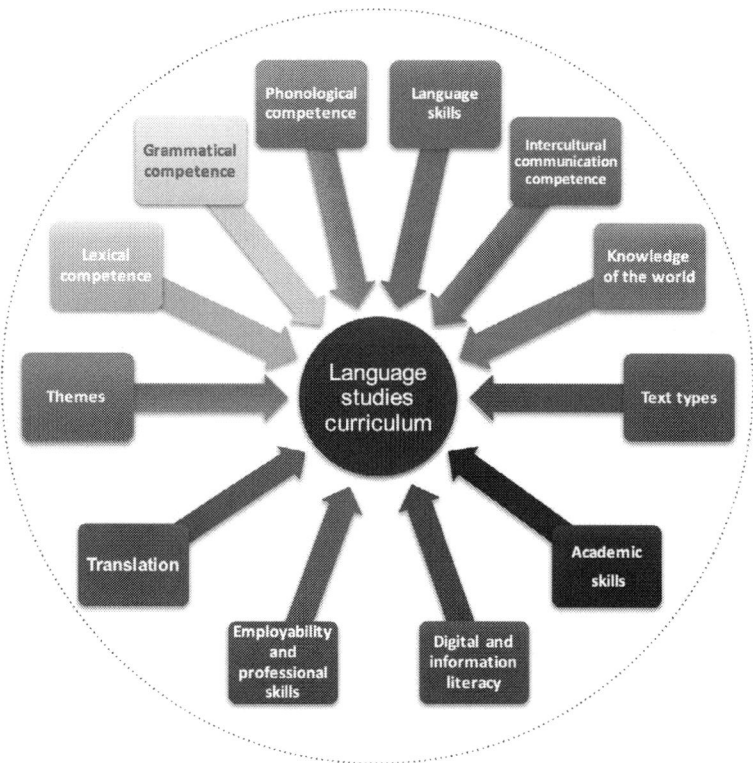

The OU's trademark model of the "teacher's voice in print" (Coleman & Vialleton, 2011, p. 235; see also Rowntree, 1994) was adjusted to ensure that the teacher in print attracted the students' attention to the various skills developed through each activity. Two examples are given below, both extracted from our module entitled *French Studies 1*, the second module studied by *ab initio* French students.

Figure 2 provides an example of a reflective question asked to students at the end of a section on traditional festivals in France, including the teaching text provided to them as a follow-up discussion prompt (The Open University, 2017b).

Figure 2. Reflective learning activity mentioning skills developed by languages graduates

Étape E

Under what circumstances might it be important to be aware of festivals or traditions from another culture? Think of at least one example. Answer in English.

Pourquoi c'est important de connaître les traditions d'autres cultures ? Répondez en anglais.

Intercultural awareness

Knowing about festivals and traditions can be useful when interacting with someone from another country: it can, for example, help avoid making cultural assumptions about how people behave or about what they do on particular occasions. By studying this unit, you are furthering your knowledge of francophone cultures, and you will get to know more about a number of festivals and traditions in French-speaking countries in Europe. Furthermore, as a language learner, you are becoming aware of the importance of not making assumptions when you communicate with people from other cultures, even when you don't have any knowledge about their specific culture. Intercultural communication skills are key skills developed by languages graduates. They are relevant in all multicultural contexts, whether it be doing business abroad, working with colleagues from a variety of cultural backgrounds, or living in a multicultural town. Flexibility, curiosity and openness are some of the characteristics developed by languages graduates, who have learned to expect different behaviours from people from different cultures.

The picture above illustrates how students are encouraged to reflect on the relevance of what they learn within the module, and the way the teaching text provides examples of how this can be articulated.

Such reflection is also embedded in the module materials through a careful selection of learning resources. For examples, in the *French Studies 1* module, we interviewed and filmed six French-speaking people, some of whom had studied languages at university. We asked them to explain to students how the skills they acquired at the time were relevant to their current careers, from teaching to nursing or shop-keeping. We then asked students to reuse the same phrases and ideas in a simulated conversation. The interviews are then also used as resources to teach a range of subject-specific learning objectives.

Furthermore, at the end of each module unit, students are encouraged to reflect on their learning, both as part of their personal development plan and to help them organise their revision work ahead of assignments. An online self-evaluation tool has been designed for this.

Figure 3 below shows an example from the same unit as above, demonstrating how students are encouraged to realise that, by being language students, they are learning skills that are desirable to employers (The Open University, 2017c). This approach trains students to articulate those attributes for themselves in whichever professional or personal context is relevant to them.

Figure 3. Self-assessment checklist and employability and professional skills for L112 unit 2

▼	Lexical competence	+/-
▼	Grammatical competence	+/-
▼	Phonological competence	+/-
▼	Language skills	+/-
▼	Translation skills	+/-
▼	Cultural knowledge	+/-
▼	Intercultural communication competence	+/-
▼	Academic skills	+/-
▼	Digital and information literacy skills	+/-
▼	Employability and professional skills	+/-

▼	Employability and professional skills	1	2	3	4	5
	I can demonstrate my ability to motivate myself: working through module materials, attending tutorials, submitting iCMA51 and TMA01.					
	I can display the ability to be an effective and self-aware independent language learner: I can work with tutor feedback.					
	I can work with grammar books and dictionaries.					
	I can organize my vocabulary and grammar notes.					
	I can analyse and assess my own strengths and weaknesses: working with the Section 5 skills checklist.					
	I understand that through intercultural awareness, languages graduates develop characteristics such as flexibility, curiosity and openness which are key employability skills.					

The first modules following the new approach were launched in 2017. A year later, our project was developed to evaluate the impact of the change. Working with ALs teaching on the modules, the project team examined how the change was perceived by them, and what their and their students' views were on the new approach.

3.   The project

A workshop with ALs who tutor on the school's languages modules was organised to share the principles behind the curriculum redesign, collect feedback from practitioners, and discuss how best to embed the development of employability skills in modules studied by students as diverse as those found at the OU.

Five ALs took part in the workshop and two were placed on a waiting list. In the end, four ALs could participate in the one-day workshop which was facilitated by three language lecturers of the School of Languages and Applied Linguistics.

In preparation of the workshop, the four participants were asked to collect statements from their students, answering two specific questions:

- Where do you think you will be using your L2 skills in the future?

- What other skills do you think you will be needing (for a job/work/ volunteering) in the future?

The workshop was organised in seven parts:

- a brainstorm activity where participants reported on what their students said about what they are looking for in a language course and what they wish to do with their language degrees;

- a presentation on the benefits of language learning;

- a group session on skills development through module materials: participants familiarised themselves with materials based on the new curriculum and, in pairs, they identified the specific 'hidden' skills that were taught or included in the activities. Participants were also able to provide feedback to authors and editors about the accessibility and the clarity of the newly written materials;

- a presentation of the new curriculum framework for languages at the OU;

- a discussion on how to define a 'well-rounded' language graduate – based on different cultural views and perspectives, participants worked on defining educational ideals by describing the traits expected of a well-rounded language graduate;

- a focus group on cultural differences, where participants exchanged ideas and the discussion was recorded; and

- a round-up in a Strengths, Weaknesses, Opportunities, and Threats (SWOT) analysis of the new curriculum framework for language modules, where participants were invited to comment on the new curriculum and how they envisaged teaching with the new materials.

Participants were asked to complete a feedback form after the workshop.

The one-day workshop was then repeated as part of a staff development programme for ALs. The second workshop took place online four months later, and was attended by 18 participants. Similar staff training takes place regularly when modules are re-designed and findings from our project can feed into these events.

The model of integrated practitioner feedback as a process, rather than collecting product-specific evaluation data at the end of the production, has proven successful in engaging ALs in reflections about language modules, and has influenced pedagogy in the early stages of writing new module materials.

Beyond influencing ALs' practice, relevant findings from the workshop were passed on to the module-writing teams of Level 2 languages courses to improve future course design. Specific changes made for the new courses include: the importance placed on language skills used for voluntary work (not just employment); the relevance of choice in language learning activities to make them relevant to each student's particular professional or personal context; and the value of explaining pedagogical reasoning to learners through introduction and activity instructions.

4.   Discussion

The feedback and reflection model as described in our article can be seen as a complex action research cycle (Lewin, 1946). Action research for language teachers has been described as follows:

> "the process begins with the identification of a concern. Then, the practitioner investigates issues related to the concern and plans and implements a change designed to address the concern. At the heart of action research is reflection: practitioners involved in action research are expected to explore what they are doing, why they are doing it and what the impact has been after doing it" (Cabaroglu, 2014, p. 80).

Whereas in the classic action research model, teachers would first notice a need or desire for change by observing their own class, in our case, the central team of academics reacted to a shift in the external demands for language graduates, placing more emphasis on employability skills. This led to implementing a change in the curriculum by influencing syllabus design for individual language courses.

The next step, evaluating change and reflecting on change, was shared between central academics and the – in our case – more peripheral teachers who had to implement the change in their own teaching (the new language materials also meant that their teaching content had changed). However, to make this change successful in all areas of teaching, the ALs needed to understand and integrate the new emphasis on skills in their own teaching. The following round of changes, implementing the findings from the evaluation process, was again conducted centrally.

5.   Contributions to the field of modern languages

Our study can offer two distinct contributions to the field of modern language teaching: (1) a model for shared action research to fit the busy lives of part-time language teachers, and (2) a model for integrating employability skills into a modern languages curriculum. We will not go in too much detail about the principles of the first model, which has been outlined above, as this is not the focus of this article. We will focus instead on the second model for successful modern languages teaching, based on an integration of employability skills into the curriculum, and which mainly relies on actions and context-relevant initiatives foregrounding the development of knowledge, skills, and attributes which usually remain implicit in languages teaching. As specialist linguists, we need to remind ourselves that what we take for granted is not necessarily understood by non-specialists. As teachers, we need to explicitly make connections for students, and train them to articulate the detailed steps of their rich learning journeys. In our framework, this was achieved through redefining the discipline holistically as a clustering of knowledge, skills, competences, and attitudes spanning 12 distinct core areas. As course designers, our key efforts to implement this went into the careful choice of learning materials and resources to support the approach, the systematic and explicit development of intercultural communication competence and non-subject-specific skills alongside the development of language-specific skills, and a pedagogic approach which supports the development of self-reflection in our students.

6.   Conclusion

It has become imperative for the languages sector to demonstrate the wide professional relevance of language learning to specialist students, and even more so to non-specialist ones, and to educate them in articulating the nuances of what language learning brings to them.

The OU's new curriculum for modern languages has redefined the discipline as a holistic cluster of knowledge, skills, and attributes. It has achieved this by emphasising the intercultural communication competence dimension of language learning and developing a pedagogic approach which encourages self-reflection and explicit training in articulating one's skills. Our project suggests that there is a need for a collaborative approach between all the practitioners involved in educating our future languages graduates for this to be successful.

We need to ensure that our language learning programmes deliver the skillful, thoughtful, and culturally-aware linguists that society needs by raising our students' awareness of their wide range of language, communication, and professional skills, and by training them to articulate the benefits they can bring to employers. By doing this, we can ensure that those well-rounded graduates are able to secure the jobs that they aspire to and deserve to get.

References

AHRC & UKRI. (2019). *The power of languages*. https://ahrc.ukri.org/documents/publications/ahrc-the-power-of-languages/

Araújo, L., Dinis da Costa, P., Flisi, S., & Soto Calvo, E. (2015). *Languages and employability*. European Commission. http://www.onevoiceforlanguages.com/uploads/2/4/6/7/24671559/jrc97544.pdf

Baumann, U., & Vialleton, E. (2017). Intercultural communicative competence and employability in the languages curriculum at the Open University UK. In E. Císlerová & M. Štefl (Eds), *Intercultural communicative competence: a competitive advantage for global employability* (pp. 35-45). Czech Technical University, Prague. http://docs.wixstatic.com/ugd/526a9b_de8f434e7f0f4f86a62a96920cef680f.pdf

Cabaroglu, N. (2014). Professional development through action research: impact on self-efficacy. *System, 44*, 79-88. https://doi.org/10.1016/j.system.2014.03.003

CBI/Pearson. (2019). *Education and learning for the modern world: CBI/Pearson education and skills survey report 2019*. https://www.cbi.org.uk/articles/education-and-learning-for-the-modern-world/

Coleman, J., & Vialleton, E. (2011). French studies at the Open University: pointers to the future. In P. Lane & M. Worton (Eds), *French studies in and for the 21st century* (pp. 235-246). Liverpool University Press. https://doi.org/10.5949/upo9781846316692.021

Kellett, M., & Clifton, G. (2017). *Measuring gains and employability for part-time students*. Wonkhe. http://wonkhe.com/blogs/analysis-measuring-gains-and-employability-for-part-time-students/

Kelly, M. (2016). Foreword. In E. Corradini, K. Borthwick & A. Gallagher-Brett (Eds), *Employability for languages: a handbook* (pp. xix-xx). Research-publishing.net. https://doi.org/10.14705/rpnet.2016.cbg2016.454

Lewin, K. (1946). Action research and minority problems. *Journal of Social Issues*, 2(4), 34-46. http://bscw.wineme.fb5.uni-siegen.de/pub/nj_bscw.cgi/d759359/5_1_ActionResearchandMinortyProblems.pdf

Rowntree, D. (1994). *Preparing materials for open, distance and flexible learning.* An action guide for teachers and trainers. In Open and Distance Learning Series. Kogan Page in association with the Open University, Institute of Educational Technology.

The British Academy. (2019). *Languages in the UK: a call for action*. https://www.thebritishacademy.ac.uk/publications/languages-uk-academies-statement/

The British Academy. (2020). *Towards a national languages strategy: education and skills.* https://www.thebritishacademy.ac.uk/publications/towards-national-languages-strategy-education-and-skills/

The Open University. (2017a). *L112: French studies 1. Module syllabus.* The Open University. Unpublished.

The Open University. (2017b). *L112: French Studies 1. Activity 2.1.2: Les fêtes marquées en France.* The Open University. Unpublished.

The Open University. (2017c). *L112: French Studies 1. Unit 2 self-assessment checklist.* The Open University. Unpublished.

Tomasson Goodwin, J., Goh, J., Verkoeyen, S., & Lithgow, K. (2019). Can students be taught to articulate employability skills? *Education and Training, 61*(4), 445-460. https://doi.org/10.1108/et-08-2018-0186

Part 2.

3 Digital transformation in education: from vision to practice during the pandemic

Paul Feldman[1]

Abstract

This contribution addresses the challenges brought on by the pandemic and argues that a forced acceleration in online teaching and assessment practices can become a sustainable model for the post-COVID-19 world. Technology is a great asset that provides learning opportunities for the whole community and the education sector should seek to adopt an innovative approach that *firmly* integrates face-to-face with virtual interaction. The effort to make the most of an unforeseen and challenging situation has brought Jisc's prediction for future learning forward: our publication *Education 4.0 Transforming the future of education through advanced technology*, offers suggestions on how this can be achieved in the current climate.

Keywords: online teaching, assessment, advanced technology, Jisc.

In March 2020, every college and university in the United Kingdom (UK) moved from almost entirely face-to-face, on-campus teaching, to fully online. In the space of three weeks, a centuries' old model was turned on its head, ready for a new term. In many ways this was an amazing success – students were being taught *en masse*, had access to most of what they needed, and were able to be assessed. Degrees were awarded and students graduated[2]. Lecturers who had been resisting the incessant march of technology were online with Microsoft Teams or Zoom with their students. Many lecturers found great new ways of

1. Jisc, London, United Kingdom; paul.feldman@jisc.ac.uk

2. https://www.universitiesuk.ac.uk/news/Pages/national-graduates-day-2020.aspx

How to cite: Feldman, P. (2021). Digital transformation in education: from vision to practice during the pandemic. In A. Plutino & E. Polisca (Eds), *Languages at work, competent multilinguals and the pedagogical challenges of COVID-19* (pp. 39-45). Research-publishing.net. https://doi.org/10.14705/rpnet.2021.49.1216

using these technologies to interact with students, to enable them to interact amongst themselves, and to really enhance their traditional teaching. We have heard of really great lecturing happening in this brave new world.

The alternative does not bear thinking about, the loss of the summer term, finalists being caught in some form of limbo etc… So, in the round we must congratulate the sector on rising to the challenges flung at it in the face of the worst crisis in most of our lifetimes. However, let us not kid ourselves that our disaster response represents a move to great online teaching. I do worry that the 'make do and mend' is seen as the way things should be. And this should not be a surprise, nor taken as a criticism. The vast majority of lecturers did not have experience of good online teaching, so they are learning as they go along. One of my favourite stories (hopefully apocryphal) is of the lecturer who wanted to scan his acetates to use for his online lectures! Many lecturers did their best to replicate their in-person teaching and were proud of what they did; however, unfortunately, great online teaching needs to be different. Very encouragingly, most institutions worked hard over the summer and the quality of 'online' teaching has grown significantly for the 2020/2021 academic year.

One of the complications we faced was online assessment. Prophetically, Jisc released a thought piece calling for a rethink of assessment[3] just before the pandemic. As students experience more flexible teaching and as the digital world intrudes ever more on the physical world (so making cheating increasingly easy and harder to spot), we see many challenges to physically present assessment and potentially less need for it. With high-stakes exams comes the need for high-quality invigilation. As we saw, when physical presence was not possible, every institution globally had to rethink how it was going to test securely; can/should this prove the start of the end of high-stakes exams? How do we build on this to accelerate what should be better ways of approaching the issue?

In the summer, students who had signed up for an on-campus, face-to-face experience were wondering why they were paying such high fees. Instead of

3. https://www.jisc.ac.uk/reports/the-future-of-assessment

being with mates, enjoying their summer term, and the occasional lecture and exams, they were back with their parents trying to get enough bandwidth to be able to do their assignments. I heard from my own nephew that he had to get up in the middle of the night to be able to have a clear enough run at downloading his project materials; a story repeated up and down the country. We have seen those concerns continue in the new academic semester (2021/2022) with the potential for a high level of dropouts given the mismatch of students' expectations and the reality of the COVID-19 world.

Jisc had been forming an exciting vision of how teaching and learning could be in the mid-2030s with the report on *Education 4.0 Transforming the future of education through advanced technology*[4]. As Jisc chief executive officer, I have been part of a team predicting the move to machine/self-directed personalised, adaptive learning, and inbuilt assessment, with face-to-face seminars. We saw our 15-year vision become, in some sense, the way things are done in 15 days (excuse the creative licence). Of course, what we are seeing is only a part of our vision, but directionally there has been a shift to make it a reality.

There is a widespread belief in university leadership, both in the UK and globally, that we must take the best out of this crisis and a determination not to return to how things were. This mirrors the much-parroted phrase to 'build back better'. Behind this is a universal belief that the crucible of necessity has forged an understanding that things can be different and that the difference works, so let us take something good out of the awfulness of the crisis.

Fortunately, few people want to adopt a purely virtual model, which we wholeheartedly agree with. Our education 4.0 vision is one where humanity prevails, where technology takes away the mundane, repeatable work, and people are freed up to interact, to discuss and debate, to challenge, and to learn together. So no more sitting in large lecture theatres purely listening (as a caricature). Instead, spending time in more tutorial/seminar settings and really getting beneath the knowledge that can adequately be imparted virtually. We

4. https://www.jisc.ac.uk/education-4-0

suggest institutions should adopt more active-based learning in embedding the online teaching, as well as enhancing students' skills and capabilities. There has been a narrative for some time that we need to give our students the 'soft' skills and the digital skills they will need in their careers, and these new models of pedagogy give that opportunity to make this happen faster and better.

While the essence of the vision is happening now – the fundamental change in the way teaching happens – key technologies that we predict are needed for the full impact are not yet ready for Higher Education (HE), in particular the use of AI (Artificial Intelligence) and mixed reality. In both these cases there are opportunities to try and learn using them now, but we need further generations of advances to happen in the capability of machine learning for AI to be able to be anywhere close to 'tutoring' a student; at the same time, on mixed reality we need much lower price points for the high-quality experience that would be needed to make it 'the norm'.

So, 2021/2022 is seeing a wide range of hybrid teaching and learning models, e.g. live lectures with both in-person and online students. We expect this to continue at least until summer 2022. One of my fears, as an optimist who hopes that good will come from the crisis, is how to embed this change. The status quo has survived hundreds of years and, once social distancing is no longer needed, it would be easier to snap back to the past to a place that 'works' rather than to persevere and build better (and we do believe that it will be better for students). Jisc is working hard to mitigate this risk!

So, what do universities need to do to improve the chance of getting a high-quality teaching student experience? A key element is to give our teaching staff the skills they need to do it well. Learning technologists had gained a good sense of what works and this has been tested in the white-hot forge of necessity in recent months. Jisc and Universities UK (UUK) are leading a highly collaborative exercise across the UK which HE called Learning & Teaching Reimagined[5]. This collaboration informed practice for the remainder

---

5. https://www.jisc.ac.uk/learning-and-teaching-reimagined

of 2020/2021, while providing key recommendations to make 2021/2022 the first of a revised and improved future of education, all within the context of a sector-leader-driven 2030 vision. I encourage you to look at the reports and the synthesis of survey findings (of students, staff, and leaders) which make fascinating reading.

At Jisc, we are prioritising our work to address these recommendations so that capacity is in place when institutions need it as the future unfolds.

It is crucial that we make the lessons we have learnt widely available and encourage adoption of revised principles by our lecturers. In some senses our recommendations should not be a surprise and I cover many of them in this piece. One we would particularly point you to in the report is to work with your students and get them to help shape the learning experiences.

A key need we are seeing widely demanded is for a step change in the skills of all university staff. This is a trend we have seen emerging strongly in recent years and the pandemic has accelerated the need. For example, our annual digital insights survey[6] pre-crisis indicated that 74% of staff did not teach online, and only 20% gave personalised digital feedback. Academic staff have done what was needed, now we need to give them the skills, knowledge, and experience they need to be great teachers in our 'new normal' world. We need examples of best practice and training in how best to use the tools at our disposal to teach our students.

Back to content, however. The UK's further education world is very comfortable working as a sector to develop content for teaching purposes – they do see their difference being in the overall student experience. We see less appetite for this in HE globally. We do believe the sector should collaborate and build seminal online teaching materials and digital artefacts at an affordable price and in a maintainable way. (Note: this is not a 'back to the future' call for open educational resources, there needs to be a sustainable financial model).

---

6. https://www.jisc.ac.uk/digital-experience-insights

This is particularly true for mixed reality. While realising the full potential of this is some way off, there are many areas where it is making a difference already, especially in 'vocational' spaces. Where space on campus is in short supply or access to labs is a precious commodity, can we use virtual reality, for example, to replicate the learning and maintain our students' pace of teaching? If so, the cost of production of credible content is so high that it probably needs consortia to make it viable.

While students have found it quite difficult to maintain engagement watching a 'Zoom' lecture, we have seen great examples of lecturers and students using the 'chat', and Q&A functions to generate a higher level of interaction than generally happened in lectures. There are pros and cons to this: are the students paying more attention to each other than the lecture, for example; behaviour that would not be acceptable in a live lecture (talking to each other loudly) is an expectation for many students when it is online. Also, when the lecture is not live (which in many spaces is the right thing to do), then human interaction is not as effective (or if it is not watched simultaneously, even possible). So, we see a key need to introduce ways for students to explore these subjects together online, especially in the coming year when on-campus time and space is at a premium.

We also need to return to the question of assessment. Much assessment happened in a 'just do it' way in 2019/2020. This is not sustainable in a 'new normal' model. We need a key debate on what assessment means in a digital world and how to do it well: our report[7] is a good starting point.

All the discussion above is, by and large, discipline agnostic; but we must not ignore the specialists' needs. The creative arts, due to their inherent physicality have experienced critical issues where we need to find solutions (e.g. how do you examine a music student online, or how do you enable drama performances with students socially distancing when even the BBC cannot keep; such as *The Archers* going as an ensemble?). Science and engineering students need access to labs and specialist equipment; much of this learning is done as project teams.

---

7. https://www.jisc.ac.uk/reports/the-future-of-assessment

And so on. All of which just underlines the challenges facing us, but what a great prize at the end!

Put this all together and institutions, and to an extent the HE sector as a whole, need to develop visions for their 'new normal' way of teaching, a vision for its digital transformation, and building on what is happened. This can be different for each university; we certainly do not want to see a homogenising of the student experience. We have a rich panoply of institutions in the UK that are exciting and drive innovation, so it is essential each organisation designs for their culture and key energising strengths.

We are living through an inflection point in history at the moment. It is in our hands to come out of this better, stronger, and with a clear path to a new way; we encourage all of you to grab the opportunity to build the HE sector for the future that our students deserve.

4 Reflections on the impact of COVID-19 on teaching and learning in the Faculty of Arts at the University of Nottingham

Cecilia Goria[1]

Abstract

It is widely believed that digitally-driven changes are not welcomed amongst academic staff in higher education. However, when in March 2020, the University of Nottingham went online in response to the UK government's COVID-19 lockdown, a different picture started to emerge. This contribution reflects on the initial steps taken to respond to the COVID-19 emergency measures, including the support required to implement these steps and ensuing staff feedback. It also reflects on the process of moving forward from a state of emergency to a more thought-through digital pedagogical approach. In this scenario, the ultimate goal of this reflection is to argue that, as a consequence of the educational turbulence caused by COVID-19, the portrait of academics prone to resisting digitally-driven changes needs to be replaced by one that emphasises the significance of making the pedagogical values of these changes meaningful to the staff who eventually implement them.

Keywords: emergency remote teaching, adapted remote teaching, institutional response, staff response, distance education.

It is commonly claimed that academics in higher education do not welcome digital changes and do not favour digital pedagogies, even though plenty of

1. University of Nottingham, Nottingham, United Kingdom; cecilia.goria@nottingham.ac.uk; https://orcid.org/0000-0002-4530-4038

How to cite: Goria, C. (2021). Reflections on the impact of COVID-19 on teaching and learning in the Faculty of Arts at the University of Nottingham. In A. Plutino & E. Polisca (Eds), *Languages at work, competent multilinguals and the pedagogical challenges of COVID-19* (pp. 47-55). Research-publishing.net. https://doi.org/10.14705/rpnet.2021.49.1217

exceptions are to be found across all disciplines. Digital changes are often perceived as an imposition by management driven by a rationale that has little to do with the quality of teaching and learning. Common complaints regard the lack of time and training required to 'do a good job', which results in the perception that adopting technology for teaching is nothing more than a gimmick to meet students' expectations. Hence, there is the belief that, with the exception of silos of excellence, academics are prone to resisting technology.

It is argued here that COVID-19 revealed a different picture. When, in March 2020, the University of Nottingham moved all its face-to-face teaching online to cope with the UK government's COVID-19 lockdown measures, academics embraced the digital change, motivated by their awareness of the benefits of technology for responding to the new situation.

In my role as Digital Learning Director of the Faculty of Arts, I became involved in the decision-making process for moving face-to-face teaching to the online environment and for drawing up a plan to support this transition. This short contribution is a reflection on aspects connected to this process: the initial steps taken to respond to the lockdown restrictions; the levels of support required to implement these steps; staff's feedback at the end of the first phase of COVID-19; the preparatory process for COVID-19's second phase in September 2020/2021; and, finally, the 'lessons learnt' regarding the commonly-alleged resistance to digital changes by academic staff.

When, in March 2020, the university moved its teaching to the online environment, many academics were caught unprepared and became rather daunted by the unfamiliar parameters of online pedagogies.

The first step taken by the university was to clarify that staff were not expected to turn into expert online pedagogues; instead, they were encouraged to respond to the new situation with realistic goals. Emergency Remote Teaching (ERT) – the quick unplanned response to the lockdown (Hodges et al., 2020) – took shape in sharp contrast with distance education in its true sense, i.e. teaching and learning planned and designed for online delivery.

A second step was to establish a package of digital tools that the university could support. Even though a mixed economy of third-party tools surfaced as the norm, the direction taken by the institution was to make use of the university-supported platforms to guarantee technical support to staff and students. As a consequence, many academics modified their practices further, adding uncertainty and workload to their ERT.

A package of platforms was recommended, reflecting directly the emerging ERT needs to:

- create asynchronous content, mainly in the form of recorded lectures (the video platform Echo360 or narrated PowerPoint);

- support student-tutor and student-student interaction (Microsoft Teams); and

- deliver instructions and host content (Moodle).

The most striking feature of ERT was the significant increase in the use of Microsoft Teams. Although its adoption had been slow in the past, academics across all faculties clearly saw the platform's high level of flexibility as an effective solution for engaging with students during ERT.

In terms of teaching structure, the Faculty of Arts prioritised the lecture+seminar format, familiar to staff and students. Thus, as a third step, academic staff adapted their teaching materials and practices to retain this structure in the digital environment.

As the lecture+seminar format does not suit language teaching – for which oral interaction, close monitoring by the tutor, and emphasis on practice, production, and performance are key – an ERT model specific for language teaching was devised. Juggling between synchronous and asynchronous delivery, a work plan was prescribed to replace the original weekly face-to-face contact hours with a weekly delivery of:

- asynchronous delivery: a video/audio file with accompanying tasks; a reading comprehension with associated tasks; a grammar point with explanations and exercises; and a writing task; and

- synchronous delivery: 30-minute live online language sessions for spoken practice.

The emphasis on asynchronous delivery proved effective in coping with the diverse and unforeseeable situations with which staff and students were confronted. However, it became apparent that a move from ERT to a more thought-through solution required a revision of the model to allow for more synchronous exchanges.

Regarding assessment, the language centre end-of-term exams were replaced by a five-day take-home exam for the lower language proficiency levels (A1-B1) – the five-day length was prescribed university-wide as an Equality, Diversity, Inclusivity (EDI) requirement – and a combination of a five-day take-home exam and a recorded oral presentation for the higher levels (B2-C1). While the oral recordings presented difficulties of technical nature, the take-home exams proved inadequate for language work, as the inability to supervise the students' performances remotely made it difficult to assess the authenticity of their work.

In spite of the generic, as well as the discipline-specific, challenges imposed by COVID-19, staff's response to ERT was remarkably constructive; academics were thrown in at the deep end, and they swam in style.

The ERT-related support began by offering technological guidance to enable academic staff to move their face-to-face teaching to the online environment. This phase was led by a team of faculty-based Digital Learning Directors (DLDs) and a centrally-based team of learning technologists, who looked for effective 'how to' solutions to ensure that teaching could continue in spite of the disruption. Little-to-no considerations were made about the pedagogy of online teaching, thus consolidating the claim that the highly instructional nature of ERT is not comparable to distance education in its true sense.

Soon, it became apparent that some academics responded positively to the centrally-led one-size-fits-all training programme, while many others felt the need for targeted instructions that matched their discipline-specific needs. Thus, a diversified multi-level model was required to provide different types of support.

A granular model was put in place to offer faculty-level, departmental-level, and on-demand individual-level training sessions, as well as daily virtual drop-in time slots to address unplanned requests.

The language centre is again a case in point highlighting the need for purposely designed support. The language teaching model outlined earlier entailed a drastic change in teaching patterns that required bespoke training on tools and practice; particular attention was paid to prepare language tutors and students to manage oral exchanges and presentations online.

In addition to granularity, all levels of training benefited from the academic expertise of the DLDs, who contributed to the planning and delivery of the support programme. In particular, the centrally organised sessions led by members of the central team of learning technologists were rehearsed with the DLDs to ensure that they met the needs and expectations of the academics, and to guarantee a joined-up approach consistent with the local training initiatives.

Three months into the COVID-19 lockdown, a Faculty of Arts unpublished staff survey report (Jarvis, 2020) was conducted in order to:

- identify features of staff's immediate response to the emergency lockdown;

- identify which platforms and tools were used for ERT delivery;

- elicit reflection on, and rate the experience of, transitioning to the online environment;

- rate student engagement, and identify methods to support it;

- consider ways to adapt assessment activities; and

- gather intelligence to inform future steps.

While it is beyond the scope of this reflection to present staff responses in detail, a few emerging themes are worth considering. A significant portion of staff was concerned with improving communication with students and accommodating their teaching to students' needs, bringing EDI concerns to the fore. In terms of level of difficulty related to ERT, on a scale 1 (easy) to 5 (difficult), 2% voted 1; 18% voted 2; 34% voted 3; 29% voted 4; and 16% voted 5.

The most common responses to the question *What worked well?* referred positively to the flexibility of the marriage between Teams and Moodle, and to the benefits of adopting a granular approach: small groups, short recordings, and shorter synchronous sessions.

To the question *What would you do differently?*, most responses mentioned the need to adapt teaching practices to increase student participation and engagement.

The most significant theme emerging from the survey, one that impacted significantly plans for the next phase of COVID-19, was the need for academics to continue to take a pragmatic approach; the need for exemplars, demonstrations of best practice, and practical guidance on how to construct suitable teaching units that combine face-to-face and online delivery scored very highly in the question related to future support.

Informed by the data gathered through the staff survey and building on the intelligence acquired through professional conversations that emerged from the multi-level support plan outlined earlier, a new approach was taken to facilitate new, flexible delivery solutions.

The measures related to the sudden lockdown in March 2020 were replaced by a much more planned transition from ERT to a pedagogically-sound teaching delivery strategy, that, while still not fully comparable to rigorous distance education, was a step forward in the right direction; it was a strategy that addressed pedagogical principles and solutions for best practice alongside technical and technological considerations.

Thus, introducing a new acronym, COVID-19's second phase saw the emergence of Adapted Remote Teaching (ART) to promote the renovation of teaching content and practices for a mixed-mode delivery, and to set goals that are realistic and achievable in the timeframe within which academics are operating. The overarching objective of ART was to support academic staff in developing their teaching building on existing resources, instead of, as some colleagues put it, 'starting from scratch'.

To support ART, the Faculty of Arts provided academics with a portfolio of examples of best practice connected to 'how to' instructions. These were framed within a set of pedagogical principles concerned with the nature and quality of the online experience of the learners and a set of related operational statements to guide the implementation of these principles. Figure 1 below illustrates the multiple paths onto which academic staff were led.

Figure 1. Support model for ART

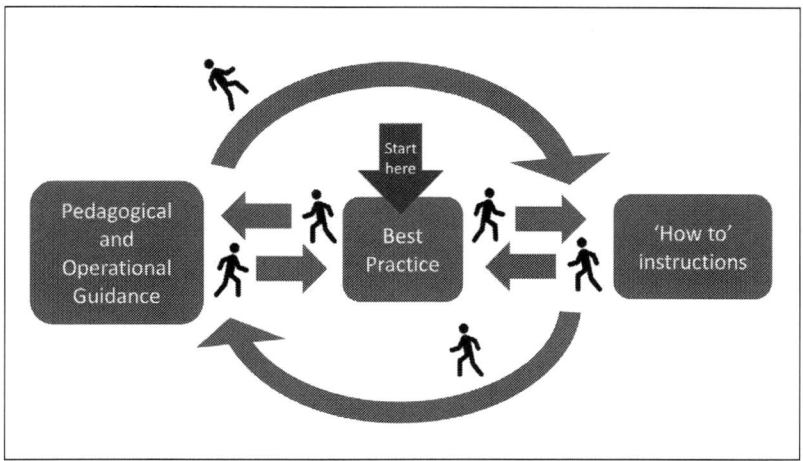

The distinctive feature of this approach rests on the centrality of best practice and the significance of providing staff with concrete examples, demonstrations, and illustrations of teaching units constructed in ways that relate directly to their practice, address their concerns, and meet their needs in practical terms. Depending on their needs, individuals are able to follow flexible bi-directional paths to access the guidance that frames the practice and the 'how to' instructions required for building their own ART.

The challenge of this approach is to ensure that all possible paths are logically signposted and coherently joined up to ensure consistency and avoid the feeling of disorientation and resource overload. To address it, a website was created to aggregate resources and increase the visibility of the paths illustrated in Figure 1.

In spite of the significant disruption, in COVID-19, as in every cloud, there is a silver lining; ERT revealed the need to review the widespread claim that academics are against change and, in particular, digital change.

The Faculty of Arts staff survey mentioned earlier and similar surveys conducted across all faculties of the university show that, under COVID-19 restrictions, academics embraced changes quickly, flexibly, and effectively. As technology became the only way to ensure the continuation of students' learning, a remarkable degree of pedagogical and technological creativity came to light. For instance, in addition to the widespread adoption of Teams to deliver live lectures and seminars, most academics readily recorded their lectures, even those who had shown reluctance to do so in the pre-COVID-19 era. The majority of these recordings were then interspersed with different forms of interactivity to ensure student engagement and participation; an aspect of 'going online' that most academics claimed they were willing to explore further.

Other examples of pedagogical changes brought on by COVID-19 came from those colleagues who opted to actively involve their students in making the transition to the online environment happen. They established an open dialogue with their students, and empowered them to shape their online learning experience. Reports from these colleagues revealed that this unprecedented student-tutor relationship based on transparency, communication, and participation facilitated the learning process and enhanced the quality of their own teaching experience.

With this in mind, I am led to reconsider the commonly-held view of change-resistant academics, especially with regard to digital change. My claim is that academic staff is open to adopting technology if and when they see its pedagogical values. ERT has shown that effective digital transformations must be based on the understanding that they bring pedagogical benefits to all constituents, students and staff alike. The error commonly made is to propose the digitalisation of education as a top-down mandate to which academics must adhere in order to satisfy students' needs and expectations.

The ART model illustrated in Figure 1 is consistent with this view; it is believed that taking best practice as the starting point for preparing academics for the second phase of COVID-19 facilitated the understanding of the pedagogical benefits of technology-enhanced teaching by speaking directly to the needs of the individuals.

To conclude, although COVID-19 has caused major disruptions in higher education, the response at the University of Nottingham has been constructive and encouraging, demonstrating the readiness of the institution and individual academics to undertake new pedagogical paths. In this light, it is hoped that this short reflection will contribute to the discourse around digital education during and beyond COVID-19.

References

Hodges C., Moore, S., Lockee, L., Trust, T., & Bond, A. (2020). The difference between emergency remote teaching and online learning. *EDUCAUSE Review*. https://er.educause.edu/articles/2020/3/the-difference-between-emergency-remote-teaching-and-online-learning

Jarvis, L. (2020). *Unpublished staff survey report.*

5 The 'go digital' Bristol experience

Gloria Visintini[1]

Abstract

This article describes the move to digital teaching and learning for the language team in the School of Modern Languages (SML) at the University of Bristol as a consequence of COVID-19 in March 2020. Topics discussed here include the educational guidelines the university put in place; how these were followed and implemented by colleagues in Modern Languages; the new digital teaching and assessment practices; how decisions were reached across languages; technologies that people used and the support available; challenges in delivering teaching; and, lastly, the opportunities created for staff and students. In describing our practice during the pandemic, I will also offer my personal take and observations as the person responsible for digital education in the Arts Faculty who assisted the language team in this transition. I will reflect on how this pandemic has accelerated our digital education agenda and how having a background in language teaching has helped and informed some of the – sometimes difficult – conversations I had with my language colleagues during these fast-moving and uncertain times. The article will end with a brief description of some of our remaining challenges and lessons learnt while the university has announced that next academic year will be delivered largely digitally. The work done so far will inform our planning.

Keywords: digital teaching and learning, staff development, digital education agenda.

1. University of Bristol, Bristol, United Kingdom; g.visintini@bristol.ac.uk

How to cite: Visintini, G. (2021). The 'go digital' Bristol experience. In A. Plutino & E. Polisca (Eds), *Languages at work, competent multilinguals and the pedagogical challenges of COVID-19* (pp. 57-62). Research-publishing.net. https://doi.org/10.14705/rpnet.2021.49.1218

Just before the national lockdown on March 13th 2020, the Vice-Chancellor and President of the university of Bristol announced that we would "move our learning and assessment online, wherever practical, as a matter of urgency".

At that point, as the person responsible for digital education in the Faculty of Arts, I was already helping the SML plan their move to online teaching. Indeed, even before the university announcement, it was becoming clear that there was a real possibility that face-to-face teaching might no longer be possible, and so I was asked by the SML Head of School to look at how they could best move to remote teaching and assessment.

It became apparent that the university wanted to adopt an institution-wide approach to this transition. In terms of teaching, the university had decided that, after the Easter break, the remaining four weeks of teaching had to be delivered entirely online. There was an acknowledgement that moving materials online would require time, so the deans and the heads of school were instructed to allow staff to prioritise preparation for online teaching over other duties and responsibilities.

The teaching had to be accessible via the institutional virtual learning environment, namely Blackboard, and each week had to include at least the following four components/steps:

- clear instructions for learning;

- an input or provocation (i.e. a synchronous live session or asynchronous slides or videos);

- a guided activity for students to complete; and

- a checkpoint/opportunity for feedback to students.

The central Digital Education Office built a website and a week-long online course, with detailed information on each component and suggestions on which technologies (alongside Blackboard) staff could use to deliver their online teaching.

In relation to assessment, the university asked academic staff to simplify and reduce their assessments, as well as to find alternative types when the existing ones could not be delivered anymore, like exams. As such, schools and centres had to completely rethink this component, as the university was now effectively moving away from unit-based assessments and adopting a more holistic and almost programme-level assessment approach.

Faculties played a key role in assisting schools and centres in their implementation of these changes. In the Arts Faculty, for example, the Education Contingency Planning Group was established to help interpret and deliver university decisions, mitigate risks, and put together new processes. The Group was co-chaired by the faculty undergraduate and postgraduate education directors, and it included staff in leadership educational roles from each school and centre, as well as myself.

As a member of the faculty Education Contingency Planning Group, I was able to offer more local and subject-specific support, and to oversee the work of academics such as my language teaching colleagues in the SML.

In terms of their transition to online delivery, academics did exceptional work in quickly rethinking their remaining teaching for the academic year. They embraced the university approach of the four components – which happened to be very similar to what I was planning for the whole school – and required little help from me or the Digital Education Office to develop their activities.

I believe that this was largely due to the clear governance of the school. Indeed, each department has a language team with a director and a deputy who make key decisions, organise work, and provide leadership. Depending on the size of the department, the teams can be comprised of five to more than ten members of staff. They all have well-defined roles and responsibilities, which have facilitated some outstanding teamwork during the coronavirus crisis.

Based on their specific learning objectives and pedagogical approaches, each team developed slightly different teaching and learning activities. But, what they all offered in a similar way were some synchronous sessions of speaking practice.

When, at the end of the teaching period, we took stock of our practice in a meeting, the main challenge language teachers reported was the lack of engagement from some of their students. Given the amount of work colleagues had put into creating the new activities, it was disappointing to see that some students did not take part. This, however, is an 'old' problem, not unique to digital delivery, typical of face-to-face teaching, as well. The question of how we can tackle this issue is now one the faculty is also looking into, to try and help all schools (and not just Modern Languages) addressing it.

Other issues identified in delivering digital teaching were that some staff and students had poor connectivity (making it especially difficult to run or attend live sessions and upload content), and did not have many technologies available to work with when creating new material.

Despite these issues, which the teams were able to overcome, the transition to online language teaching went smoothly. Less straightforward, on the other hand, was the switch to online assessment. Pre-pandemic, the language teams relied heavily on paper exams to evaluate student language acquisition. As this kind of exam could no longer take place, language teams were asked to come up with alternative methods and simplify their assessments.

As a result, some assessments were dropped, and others were reworked. For instance, the oral exams (when kept) were replaced by a student-produced video 8-to-10 minutes in length. For compositions and guided writing elements, language colleagues put forward the case for timed online exams, where students had only a few hours to complete their assessment. However, the University (myself included) felt these were too risky, and could discriminate against those students working in difficult circumstances and with poor connectivity, who might struggle to access, complete, and submit the exam within a short timeframe.

This stance sparked some difficult conversations. In the end, it was felt that the way forward to test student remote learning was through open-book exams, where students had five working days to complete and submit their exam.

While this timeframe was fairer on students, the downside was that they could access notes and online resources while taking the assessment, which, when you test knowledge or skill acquisition instead of reasoning, can lead to inflated results. The other downside of open-book exams was that they were not supported by the Central Exam Office and required completely new processes – scheduling the exams, making them available to students, and promoting an updated code of conduct, etc. – which were led by the faculty in collaboration with schools and centres.

Whether we will be using open-book exams for language assessment in the future still remains to be seen. Given all their limitations, what they have shown, however, is that the school can move away from paper exams. Colleagues in SML had been talking about changing the format of language assessments for years, and, while they were making some progress towards this, the pandemic has certainly accelerated that process.

The pandemic has also speeded up our process of upskilling some colleagues in their use of technologies. For example, all language colleagues are now familiar with webinar and conferencing tools, and have shifted to marking assessments online. These were all items that had been on our list of things to organise for a number of years, but kept getting pushed back for various reasons (e.g. lack of time and resources, the false perception that languages can best be taught face-to-face, and that some language work is too complex to be marked online).

In planning the post-COVID academic year, which will be largely delivered online by the faculty, we have decided to revamp and modernise our Blackboard sites by introducing a new visual look and a common structure in order to offer a more pleasant environment and better functionality for the virtual classroom. For language staff, this translates into populating their sites with newly designed teaching and learning activities.

Some of them are eager to use new technologies and develop more innovative and cutting-edge language work. Indeed, some language colleagues have been experimenting with technologies for years, presenting their work at national and international conferences. It would be a pity not to facilitate such passion for innovation, and a shame not to give colleagues the particular tools they need to produce outstanding work. This is something that I hope I can better support this time, unlike at the start of the COVID-19 crisis, when there was a clear effort from the university to adopt institutionally supported technologies wherever possible.

I am also hoping that we, as a faculty, will have more time to collect systematic and meaningful feedback from staff and students, beyond our standard end-of-the-academic-year meeting. Yet again, this is something we were unable to do well last semester because of the fast-moving situation, the fact that other priorities took over, and the need for new procedures to be organised quickly. Many colleagues and institutions will certainly recognise themselves in the fast-paced and pressurised working mode which had to be adopted during COVID-19, acknowledging that, although some informal feedback has been collected, it is now paramount to do much more on this front at every level of organisations if institutions are serious about growing and learning from their own mistakes and successes.

6 Teaching and learning post pandemic

Dale Munday[1]

Abstract

This article aims to offer one perspective on ways that Lancaster University supported its staff in the rapid shift to online teaching and learning in the midst of a global pandemic. The approach centred around the upskilling of staff, with mixed engagement across the suite of support tools and resources, which can be compared to similar situations in the wider Higher Education (HE) sector. A focus on the future of curriculum design and the associated requirements at an institutional- and sector-wide level is addressed in relation to the opportunities and challenges with which we are faced.

Keywords: digital teaching, pedagogy, online learning, digital curriculum.

When HE institutions (and effectively the entire education sector) went into lockdown, there was an immediate and emergency response to shift to an online delivery model for the remaining timetabled academic year. At Lancaster University, this brought about a dramatic shift in the traditional teaching and learning approaches that dominated the institution. The *COVID-19 Online Teaching and Learning Community* was set up using Microsoft Teams with the intention of being a rapid-response support mechanism for staff who would have a range of questions around both technical and pedagogic approaches to the new delivery model.

1. Lancaster University, Lancaster, United Kingdom; d.munday@lancaster.ac.uk; https://orcid.org/0000-0002-0412-7864

How to cite: Munday, D. (2021). Teaching and learning post pandemic. In A. Plutino & E. Polisca (Eds), *Languages at work, competent multilinguals and the pedagogical challenges of COVID-19* (pp. 63-69). Research-publishing.net. https://doi.org/10.14705/rpnet.2021.49.1219

With teaching and assessment being the most challenging scenarios to adapt in the emergency situation, my role as a digital learning facilitator placed me in a position to observe the disparity in the sector's expectations for current pedagogic practices and the level of digital capabilities attained by academic staff, who were expected to effectively shift to online teaching almost overnight. Much of the early research into digital capabilities in HE has focused on the skills and experiences of students with little emphasis on teaching staff, therefore leaving a gap in need of filling at a fast pace, given the unprecedented scenario.

Initially, the majority of queries and posts added by academic staff on the Teams *COVID-19 Online Teaching and Learning Community* group centred around the technical aspects of the technology with which they were being asked to engage. The university produced a Minimum Expectations document, which was intended to give staff a baseline to work from, directing them to institutionally supported technologies with a sound pedagogic underpinning, e.g. lectures broken down into 15-minute pre-recorded videos using one of three institutionally supported tools (Microsoft Stream, eStream, and Panopto). The intent throughout the early phases of the *COVID-19 Online Teaching and Learning Community* was to reframe the technical questions into a more pedagogic discussion to shift the mindset of teaching staff. This worked at times, with some staff taking on the pedagogy-first approach to learning design. Yet, the majority were still in fire-fighting mode, wanting quick solutions to the more technical aspects of their work with which they were unfamiliar. Who can blame them? The staff were thrust into a scenario where their day-to-day teaching practices and competence was completely turned upside down. Jisc's (2019) digital experience insights survey highlighted that 74% of HE teaching staff had never taught in an online environment, with only 27% suggesting they had received guidance about the digital skills they are expected to have as a teacher. Aware of the clear need for staff support, Lancaster University created and facilitated the *How to teach online* course, which was delivered over three weeks with live sessions, asynchronous discussions, and pre-designated reading and revision materials. 64 staff (5%) participated in the course over two cycles of delivery. When compared to the 1,190 full-time academic staff, 5% of the staff seems somewhat insignificant, especially when compared to the sector average of 74% who have not experienced online teaching. The feedback from those participating in the two cycles was complimentary, yet the overall impact when looking at the scale of attendance is disappointing. Although the quick shift to online delivery meant that more, if not all, staff had now experienced online delivery, it remained more of a 'lift and shift' approach. Standard approaches were to be over-reliant on the virtual learning environment, which at Lancaster University is Moodle, placing the focus on students accessing reading and on a heavily asynchronous approach to their learning.

When the impact that COVID-19 has had on changing the immediate landscape of HE teaching, learning, and assessment is considered, it is difficult to ignore the levels of teaching staff's competence in both designing and delivering a more digitally-centric/enabled curriculum. The institutional focus of online self-study courses has historically been aimed at the administrative functions of the various tools available, with 31% of the 7,816 courses (circa August 2019) available at Lancaster University completed by staff. Additionally, teaching-specific professional development aligns with the Higher Education Act (HEA) fellowship routes and the institution's *Post Graduate Certificate in Academic Practice* programme, which are limited in their focus on digital education and TEL. My role as a digital learning facilitator is aimed at bridging the gap between the teaching and the technology, and allows me to have a holistic overview of skills and confidence levels when it comes to TEL and curriculum design. I have seen, first hand, the chasm of the digital skills gap and the disparity between those comfortable and innovative in their approaches to Technology-Enhanced Learning (TEL) and curriculum design for the 2020/21 academic year and those who, with weeks to go until the start of the academic year, were still lacking the basic design and practical skills to create an engaging experience in what is sure to have been a challenging time for students and staff alike. Although the institution created numerous support approaches to bridge the gap between the innovators and those more accustomed to traditional analogue approaches to teaching, learning, and assessment, the issue persists. I have been enthused by the engagement of some academic staff who really focused their summer on upskilling as much as possible, attending various development opportunities, and reaching out for support and guidance. Yet there are still large numbers of staff who remain of concern, yet to engage with the resources afforded to them, potentially going into the new academic year with the mentality that the emergency remote shift may be considered an example of good practice and will only be accepted as a temporary measure for teaching students in the year ahead.

Is this then a watershed moment for digital pedagogy? I believe it can be, but only if we leave behind the 'quick fix' approach, and stop seeing digital education forevermore as the back-up when all else fails. What we have now is an opportunity to enter a prolonged dialogue with senior institutional figures and sector leaders to underline the importance of future-proofing our approach to teaching, learning, and assessment.

Entering an environment where the traditional lecture in a large lecture theatre is almost incomprehensible and logistically challenging, we may have missed a real opportunity to redefine what HE education can be. At Lancaster University, the guidance to staff for a successful transition to online or a blended delivery model was to have lectures pre-recorded and broken down into 15-minute bitesise chunks. It is agreed that this seems more suitable to digital learning than the longwinded 60-minute recordings; however, a fundamental rethink on the pedagogic purpose of the lecture was not engaged in. Assessment proved a particularly demanding issue, in which rapid decisions had to be made and assessment tasks revised and migrated online, which impacted the assessment methods used and the nature of feedback given. Longstanding issues surrounding the provision of timely and effective feedback to students prior to COVID-19 exist, yet students' thinking is often dominated by assessment and marks, rather than feedback and developmental impact. Contemporary research points towards a need to change the educational practices to focus on assessment *for* learning, opposed to assessment *of* learning, which is prevalent in the sector; however, the fallout from the pandemic has yet to really impact this. Educators are often hesitant to alter formal assessments, such as examinations and summative tests, because changing these practices places demands on time, energy, and resources.

Reshaping teaching, learning, and assessment in the HE sector is no easy task, yet, with collective buy-in and a genuine focus on student development and shift away from external metrics and league tables, I believe it can be done. A starting point for all new courses and re-validation of existing programmes should be a hybrid-first model. By this, I mean developing a type of curriculum that is multifaceted and effective across both online and face-to-face delivery. It is unlikely that this pandemic will be the only major hurdle we have to face as a sector in the coming years, so starting the process now is vital. The technology and digital infrastructure available now offer opportunities for authentic assessment and feedback practices to be embedded in the curriculum, connecting the digital classroom beyond the confines of the physical classroom or campus.

Technology in education is often seen as a management tool, serving a purpose of maintaining records, etc., but there is so much more to it. We now have the capacity to integrate 21st century skills and graduate attributes into the design of learning and really prepare students for the world after HE. To achieve this, a real determination is required to support teaching and support staff by equipping them with the relevant skills and training. Having self-help guides, tutorials, and short courses are a great start to this process, but digital pedagogy must be given the same prevalence and respect as traditional face-to-face teaching. An example to kickstart this would be for the UK Professional Standards Framework for supporting teaching and learning to progress on from asking for cases of the 'use and value of appropriate learning technologies' forming part of the HEA fellowship process and, instead, align this more throughout the criteria when discussing learning design, evidence-informed approaches, and the engagement with continuing professional development, which often leads to a subject-specific focus. Additionally, a rethink of assessment approaches that are more incremental throughout an academic year and not so summatively loaded would encourage innovation in learning design.

A shift in feedback methods which utilise the technological affordances beyond simply electronic text and upload is also a fundamental requirement. Audio and audio-visual feedback have been seen to have positive implications on students' engagement and understanding, yet fail to be widely used in HE. Engaging students in dialogue and creating a rapport through technology is possible, but often avoided by staff due to the lack of digital skills or fear of the unknown.

Many institutions are trapped in a cycle of being 'comparable' and 'benchmarked' against similar institutions, but neglect their opportunities to innovate, lead, and develop. I believe that the most successful universities emerging from the COVID-19 pandemic will be those that reacted quickly to put measures in place to plan for a changed environment post pandemic. Those that are still hoping to return to the 'old normal' will be shocked and saddened at the realisation than the old normal does not exist; the sector and educational landscape have changed forever. Now they must decide if they will embrace or fight against that change.

In regard to the specific case of Lancaster University's *COVID-19 Online Teaching and Learning Community*, its success as an efficient and effective method of dissemination and support has led to the community being rebranded the digital education network. It continues to offer support and guidance, as well as structured webinars and training sessions around digital teaching practices. In addition to this, the rapid creation of an 'embrace digital' website has offered staff a range of guidance and support for digital practice in the short- and medium-term future starting from 2020/21. A core feature within this is the creation of 'teaching formulas' which are guides of effective pedagogy, practices, and resources with step-by-step instructions for self-directed learning. In the current situation, the beliefs of post-digital scholars (Bayne & Jandrić, 2017; Feenberg, 2019, p. 8; Jandrić et al., 2018) that there is no longer a binary separation between the digital and physical world, with the two entwined in our everyday lives, is becoming ever more real.

References

Bayne, S., & Jandrić, P. (2017). From anthropocentric humanism to critical posthumanism in digital education. In P. Jandrić (Ed.), *Learning in the age of digital reason* (pp. 195-212). Sense. https://doi.org/10.1007/978-94-6351-077-6_9

Feenberg, A. (2019). Postdigital or predigital? *Postdigit Sci Educ, 1*, 8-9. https://doi.org/10.1007/s42438-018-0027-2

Jandrić, P., Knox, J., Besley, T., Ryberg, T.,Suoranta, J., & Hayes, S. (2018). Postdigital science and education. *Educational Philosophy and Theory, 50*(10), 893-899. https://doi.org/10.1080/00131857.2018.1454000

Jisc. (2019). *Digital experience insights survey 2019: findings from students in UK further and higher education.* https://www.jisc.ac.uk/reports/digital-experience-insights-survey-2019-students-uk

Locked down, but not isolated: Twitter collaboration among teachers in response to COVID-19

Fernando Rosell-Aguilar[1]

Abstract

This piece looks at the use of Twitter to share good practice among education professionals responding to the so-called 'pivot online': the sudden shift to online learning necessitated by the spread of the Coronavirus pandemic. It presents a general overview on how Twitter provided a source of advice, ideas, and resources and how teachers shared their expertise at this time of need, focusing on my own experience as a Twitter user and online pedagogy expert.

Keywords: professional development, support, online learning, social media, Twitter, community of practice.

"There's a special providence in the fall of a sparrow. If it be now, 'tis not to come. If it be not to come, it will be now. If it be not now, yet it will come – the readiness is all" (Shakespeare, Hamlet, Act 5, Scene 2).

It was like Mount Vesuvius giving signs that it was about to erupt and the people of Pompeii thinking they had nothing to fear. Despite taking a number of weeks for the coronavirus to spread from the east to the west, everyone was unprepared. As a migrant who has been a long-time resident in the United Kingdom (UK), I felt that, even as it hit continental Europe and countries such as Italy and Spain went into lockdown, the UK Government acted as though

1. University of Warwick, Coventry, United Kingdom; fernando.rosell-aguilar@warwick.ac.uk; https://orcid.org/0000-0001-9057-0565

How to cite: Rosell-Aguilar, F. (2021). Locked down, but not isolated: Twitter collaboration among teachers in response to COVID-19. In A. Plutino & E. Polisca (Eds), *Languages at work, competent multilinguals and the pedagogical challenges of COVID-19* (pp. 71-77). Research-publishing.net. https://doi.org/10.14705/rpnet.2021.49.1220

Britons could somehow be immune to the virus. Still, the virus came, the country – eventually – went on lockdown, and (with the exception of some schools providing childcare for essential workers) all educational institutions shut their doors.

The obvious decision was to move all teaching online. After all, just about every school, college, and university has a Virtual Learning Environment (VLE) – they may as well use it. But, hang on, were they not using it already? Well… yes. Sort of. Alas, despite the many collaborative tools that VLEs offer, many institutions were using them just as a place to publish timetables, class materials, and links to supplementary resources, not as teaching spaces. At best, 'online learning' in those institutions meant that students were being asked to undertake some sort of individual activity online to inform what happened in the face-to-face classroom, using a flipped learning approach.

One consequence of the COVID-19 lockdown was a considerable rise in the use of Synchronous Computer-Mediated Communication (SCMC) technologies for work and leisure purposes. Almost overnight, videoconferencing (Zoom, Skype, FaceTime, WhatsApp video) became the essential tool for staying in touch with family and friends, leading to an enormous acceleration in the normalisation process of this type of technology. From children to grandparents, meeting online became 'The New Normal'. However, knowing how to use a technology for a work meeting or hosting a quiz night does not equate to knowing how to use it for pedagogical purposes.

The directive from management was clear: "move all teaching online". Teachers who had never taught a lesson outside a physical classroom had to learn how to use SCMC tools such as Blackboard Collaborate, Adobe Connect, or Big Blue Button for live sessions with students. In many cases, institutions provided some instructions on how to use the technology, but little or no training on the best pedagogical practices in such environments. As a consequence, many teachers turned to social media to find how best to use these tools, leading to hashtags such as #onlinepivot and #onlinelearning becoming very popular in educators' timelines.

Some very useful advice came from experts in online pedagogy. Simon Horrocks (@horrocks_simon) was one of those experts leading the way, suggesting that institutions follow the advice of those who had taught online before (Figure 1).

Figure 1. Tweet by Simon Horrocks on 11/03/2020[2]

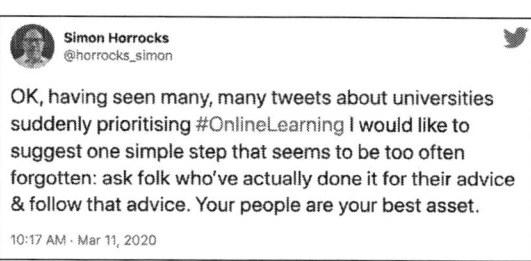

It is often assumed that students own a laptop or computer, and that they have an internet connection. Neil Mosley (@neilmosley5) made the point of not making assumptions about this (Figure 2). In my own experience, the students I was teaching (third year undergraduate and master's students at a traditional face-to-face university) did not own such devices. They normally used the many pieces of equipment and wi-fi available on campus, and their only device was a smartphone with limited data available on their phone contracts. This had a huge effect on what software they could use and for how long.

My own response to the plea from many teachers in my Twitter network for help with teaching online was to record a series of 13 short videos giving advice on how to manage SCMC environments for teaching (see Figure 3 for the first tweet in the thread). Having worked at a distance learning university for nearly 18 years before moving to a face-to-face university, I have both taught and trained many teachers to teach online, and I wanted to share the knowledge I had gained in that time in the hope that it would help teachers unfamiliar with synchronous online teaching. Knowing that the attention span for social media videos tends to lower significantly after one or two minutes, I aimed to keep the maximum length at 60 seconds.

2. https://twitter.com/horrocks_simon/status/1237668898901831680

Figure 2. Tweet by Neil Mosley on 16/03/2020[3]

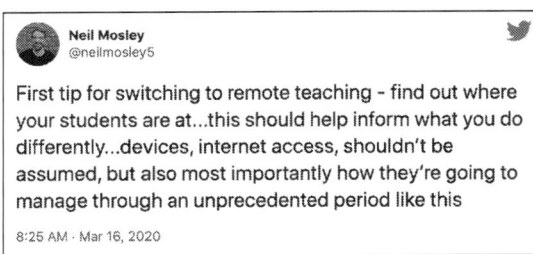

Figure 3. Tweet by Fernando Rosell-Aguilar on 19/03/2020[4]

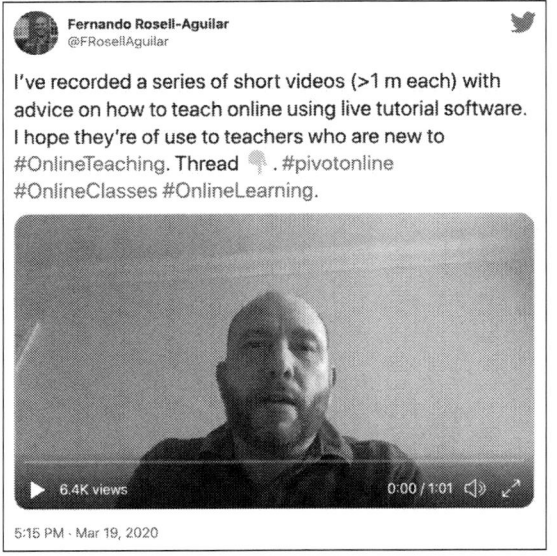

My first piece of advice was to avoid the temptation to have everyone's cameras on. As is the case with so many online tools, just because you can use it, does not mean you should. Online video consumes a lot of bandwidth, and can affect the quality of the audio for participants with weaker connections, so, after a

---

3. https://twitter.com/neilmosley5/status/1239452832400576512

4. https://twitter.com/FRosellAguilar/status/1240673255549292545?s=20

couple of minutes for greetings, checking that everyone can hear, and fostering the sense of community that seeing one another provides (particularly in the middle of a health crisis), my advice is to turn it off. This is also for pedagogical reasons, as online video can be incredibly distracting in a lesson; participants can be easily distracted by something in the background, movement, or the facial expressions of others.

The following four videos focused on the fact that the learning experience online is not the same as face-to-face, and therefore teachers should not aim to replicate what they normally do, but think about how technology can help them meet their learning outcomes. Part of this involves 'classroom' management; arranging groups or giving instructions takes longer in the online environment, and this should be taken into account during lesson planning. Instructions should be very clear and, if possible, presented on screen. I also suggested that any lecture-type content should be pre-recorded and made available prior to synchronous contact time, which should be the time for interaction among teacher and students or for students among themselves. Another piece of advice was to make sessions relatively short, as online teaching is very tiring.

The next three videos focused on the use of the SCMC technology. First of all, I suggested being upfront with learners about the fact that a teacher may be new to online learning. I also recommended establishing a procedure for what to do in case of connection problems, and not letting an individual participant's technical problems take up everyone else's time.

Because many teachers feel pressure to get everything right – a tall order in any situation – I decided to post some of the 'bloopers' and mistakes I had made whilst recording the videos. When people watch a video, they rarely think about how many attempts it may have taken to get to the piece they are watching. I wanted to show that I also get things wrong, and that is OK.

The response to the series of tweets was very positive, with thousands of video views and many replies expressing thanks for the advice. Receiving 'likes' and being retweeted by fellow teachers, professors, and organisations, such as the University Council for Modern Languages, was pleasing, but the most rewarding response was from teachers letting me know that they actually had implemented the advice I had given, and it had improved their experience of online teaching.

The tweets were also picked up outside the UK. As a result of the thread, I was interviewed for the US-based *Teacher Talking Time* podcast, which gave me an opportunity to discuss the points I had made more in-depth.

My advice was not only for teachers, though. In a separate thread, I also advised universities to invest in pedagogical training of their staff and to also train their students on issues such as time management, motivation, community development, peer support, and coping with isolation.

Of course, I was not the only one providing advice. I have, in the past, written about teacher use of hashtags providing opportunities for the creation of communities of practice where ideas, advice, and resources are shared. The #MFLTwitterari community responded actively, and shared many resources, both on Twitter and on Facebook (the Modern Languages Teachers' Lounge provided a repository for many of these – see Figure 4).

In a time of need, social media provided an environment for just-in-time professional development, and I was happy to be part of the many teachers who shared their expertise. However, this does not make up for the fact that the government and most institutions were not ready for the shift to online learning. We simply do not know how long restrictions related to COVID-19 will be in place for or when the next pandemic will come. It is too soon to tell how the lockdown teaching experience will affect tutorial provision in schools or higher education. It is unlikely that schools will adopt it in the long term, but higher education institutions have seen that their teachers and students can, for the most part, adapt to the online environment. This rise in online teaching beyond distance learning institutions may well lead to an increase in blended or full distance learning from institutions that did not provide such options before for a number of reasons, including cost and health safety.

Figure 4. The Modern Languages Teachers' Lounge on Facebook[5]

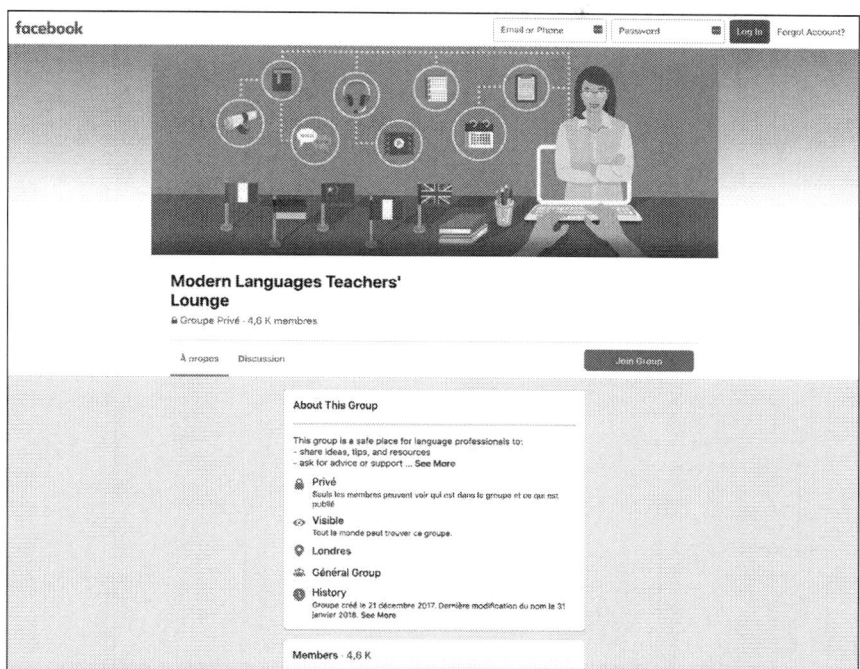

Training teachers to teach online has long been advocated, but it is now a necessity. This must be reflected in the curricula of teacher training programmes, so that everyone is ready for it. *The readiness is all*.

Acknowledgements

I would like to thank the editors for inviting me to contribute this piece. I would also like to thank Simon Horrocks and Neil Mosley for granting permission to reproduce their tweets.

---

5. https://www.facebook.com/groups/modernlanguageteacherslounge

8 Complexity and simplicity during COVID-19: reflections on moving pre-sessional programmes online at pace

Kate Borthwick[1]

Abstract

This article describes how a complex and large Pre-Sessional (PS) programme at the University of Southampton (UoS) moved online at pace during the COVID-19 pandemic. It outlines the scale of the challenge and the ideas that informed our approach. It gives an overview of the technical and learning design used to deliver the programme, and makes observations on how this was achieved using Blackboard, MS Teams, and Padlet. It indicates how a mix of whole-cohort content and smaller, online group spaces within one site were used to recreate a personalised, small-group teaching experience. It closes with some comments on lessons learned from the experience.

Keywords: pre-sessional, online learning, English language, international students.

UoS PS is a study skills and English language programme[2] designed to prepare international students for academic success in UK higher education. It runs over the summer from June to September, and has grown every year; in 2019, it welcomed over 2,200 international students from a range of countries. The majority of the students come from China, and go on to study a range of disciplines within the University at the undergraduate and postgraduate levels.

1. University of Southampton, Southampton, United Kingdom; k.borthwick@soton.ac.uk; https://orcid.org/0000-0003-2251-7898

2. https://www.southampton.ac.uk/courses/pre-sessional-language-courses.page

How to cite: Borthwick, K. (2021). Complexity and simplicity during COVID-19: reflections on moving pre-sessional programmes online at pace. In A. Plutino & E. Polisca (Eds), *Languages at work, competent multilinguals and the pedagogical challenges of COVID-19* (pp. 79-87). Research-publishing.net. https://doi.org/10.14705/rpnet.2021.49.1221

Students are typically required to pass the PS in order to progress onto their programme of study.

The summer PS programme consists of several full-time, intensive courses of study.

- Two 11-week courses in general academic English (suitable for students intending to study in any discipline) and in Business English (suitable for students intending to study in the UoS Business School). These courses are known as PSA and PSA Business.

- Two 6-week courses in general academic English and in Business English (for students with a higher IELTS[3] score[4]). These courses are known as PSB and PSB Business.

Teaching in the programme is task-based and takes place in organised, small groups, which enables a personalised learning experience. Between 150 and 250 experienced English for academic purposes tutors are recruited seasonally to deliver teaching, with many returning to Southampton each summer.

Experienced staff and well-established processes allow us to work with this large number of students, whilst tutors ensure that the programme runs smoothly and prepares students for their entries into academic and student life at Southampton. 2020, however, was shaping up to present this complex, efficient, and successful system with some challenges.

In late February 2020, I was called to a senior-level meeting to discuss a developing crisis; a disease called COVID-19 had shut down China, the country of origin for many of the university's international students. No one was travelling. No one was studying. No one was taking English language tests. The

---

3. IELTS: International English Language Testing System. It is an exam which tests proficiency in English and is an accepted measure of linguistic capability for entry to UK Universities. https://www.ielts.org/

4. Students applying for PSA and PSA Business are required to have IELTS 5.5. Students applying for PSB and PSB Business are required to have IELTS 6.0.

university was facing the prospect of losing a large number of its international students for the 2020/2021 academic year, as well as a significant chunk of income. The first place we would feel the impact of all this would be on our summer PS programmes.

The situation seemed stark: would it be necessary to cancel the PS programme with all the attendant impact that would have? Alternatively, could the whole programme be delivered online? Would a move online give our students the language support they needed? And, could this be done in time?

As director of the university's open online courses, my response was always going to be "yes!". My colleagues responsible for delivering the PS in the Academic Centre for International Students were of the same mind.

The most significant challenge in moving such a large and complicated programme online was time. PSA would launch at the end of June, and this gave us three months for planning, course/content creation, and staff familiarisation with the new arrangements and training. It is worth noting that, when I plan a new massive open online course, I schedule at least 12 months' preparation.

As the COVID-19 pandemic steadily spread and worsened in early March, all staff working on the PS programme moved to remote working from home. This situation complicated communications, decision-making, and working speed.

We also faced the prospect that our temporary tutors would have to work remotely from their own homes. This meant the immediate consideration of their Information Technology (IT) capabilities and needs in the delivery of online education.

The PS programme does not only prepare students for academic study, it also plays a key role in preparing students for social and academic life at the university. For many students, the PS programme is the first meaningful, sustained interaction they will have with the University. It also provides them with an on-location, immersive language-learning experience.

If students are studying the PS programme online from home, those aspects either cannot be delivered or may not be necessary until the time when students can arrive in person. However, an online version of the course should still aim to build community-feeling, convey a sense of welcoming, and introduce the university.

The overarching aim in our planning was to reduce unnecessary complexity and 'keep it simple'. These ideas informed our approach:

- retain the existing pedagogical approach of the PS around personalised, small-group teaching as a way of maintaining quality in the educational experience of students;

- emphasise that learning outcomes and study load expectations were unchanged;

- use existing platforms, processes, and systems, adapting them for online delivery, as well as identifying and solving any issues in real-time as we worked; and

- accept no diminishment in quality of teaching/learning due to moving online.

At Southampton, we use Blackboard[5] as our virtual learning environment to support campus-based learning. In early 2020, we were about to commence work on a series of upgrades to improve our installation of the software, including moving the site 'to the cloud' and adding Collaborate, a virtual classroom tool. This work would complement ongoing enhancements of our digital systems through the increasing use of Microsoft Office 365 and its Teams[6] app.

---

5. https://www.blackboard.com/

6. https://www.microsoft.com/

In response to the COVID-19 crisis, the work on these systems was accelerated and prioritised, which meant that the PS team felt it had the tools to deliver an effective educational experience.

Blackboard is usually used in a supporting role for the pre-sessional courses, but, in moving the programme online, it became the main means of delivering teaching and the first, principal point of contact for students. This necessitated a re-conceptualisation of how the PS Blackboard sites were used and presented.

A 'home page' was created, which would act as the default landing page – the point of entry into the course as a whole. It was given a bespoke look, with banners and colourful icons. Each icon linked through to a key area of course activity, e.g. information about the course, main course content, student support information, etc. A bespoke course menu was created to prioritise course activities and to render navigation as easy and transparent as possible. The aim of doing this was to present a welcoming online face to students and create an organised way to navigate content.

Information 'About the course' was positioned first, as this section gave information on how to navigate the online space, what to do if technical issues occurred, and also how the online course would work pedagogically (e.g. how to submit assignments or course expectations for study time and engagement). This scaffolding support was important to convey how the course works practically and technically, and to frame the educational expectations of learner and tutor. Usually, this kind of information is given verbally in class, and reinforced in downloadable course handbooks, then discussed informally with classmates and tutors. In the online space, such scaffolding of information and clarity of presentation aims instead to address the absence of social and informal information exchange.

Core course content was created for each week, and placed in a specific section on Blackboard. This material was created by the PS leadership and coordination team, and consisted of a range of materials including tasks, videos, and texts.

This material could be accessed and used by tutors in synchronous classroom sessions, and also used by students in self-study time.

Finally, a whole-cohort social area was added using a Padlet wall. This area aimed to encourage social interaction between students prior to travelling to the UK to study, and was intended to address the absence of face-to-face social exchanges (Figure 1).

Figure 1. PSA landing page

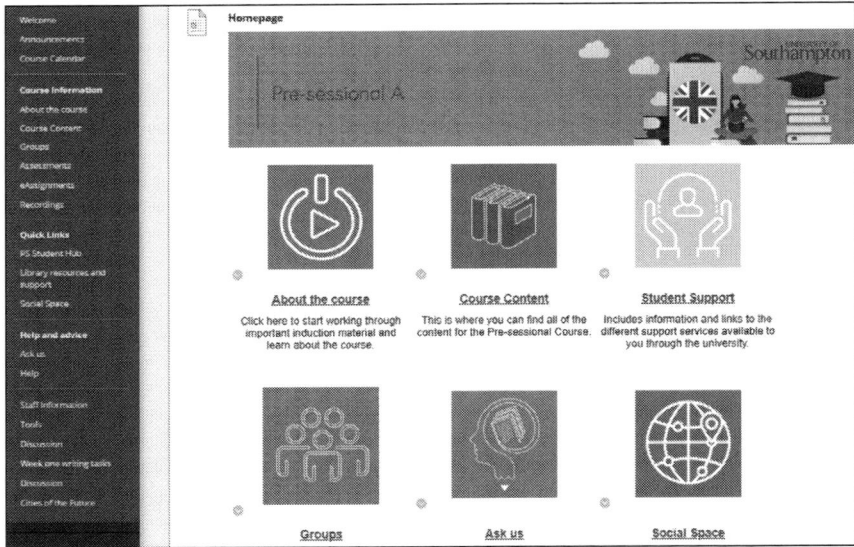

A key aspect of the pedagogical approach in the PS programme is small-group focus. Teaching, community building, and personal support is delivered through small-group interaction. Working with one Blackboard site and a large number of tutors with editing rights proved to be a technical challenge. We needed a space which could host overarching, whole-cohort information and content, but which could also have specific areas to which tutors could add resources and conduct group-specific activities.

This was achieved by making group spaces within the main Blackboard site. Each group space had its own discussion forum, Collaborate room, course folder, and separate group email function. This enabled tutors to manage their group space as they would their campus-based classroom by encouraging the sharing of class-specific resources, communication with group members, and the holding of synchronous discussions/lessons. Tutors could manage this space and their interactions as they wished. Tutors could also use this space to 'troubleshoot' issues of linguistic or content-related understanding, and also monitor attendance or uncover issues related to technical or course processes.

The PS programme maintained a high number of synchronous teaching sessions using both MS Teams and Collaborate with students. These 'live' sessions were essential in providing language practice in listening and speaking.

The mix of small-group space and live interaction aimed to supply an element of the interactive language experience students would be missing by not being in Southampton in person. Delivering an online course entirely through the medium of English provides a different kind of immersive language experience in itself – one that shifts in emphasis from oral and aural communication to reading and writing. The group spaces were intended to assist us in identifying issues in understanding and working on personalised solutions.

As I write this, the PS programmes have just drawn to a close. Over 1,500 students have taken the programme this year, and it is clear that they have engaged actively with tutors and online content. Outcomes in achievement are in line with previous years.

Robust induction programmes for tutors and students worked well in uncovering and solving technical issues with using Blackboard and Teams. As the course has progressed, we have experienced remarkably few technical issues – although we have not yet undertaken a full analysis. The course and its delivery model now exist as a repurposable entity, and, in this light, it will run again almost immediately to support international students in the Autumn of 2020.

Evaluative work on PS 2020 is just beginning as I write. However, I hope that my observations on the process of moving the PS programmes online so far might be of help to other colleagues with the need or desire to move an entire course programme from Face to Face (F2F) to online delivery.

My recommendations are:

- keep learning outcomes in focus, and stand firm on them. Teaching and learning can be just as effective online as on campus;

- maintain a good number of interactive, live classroom sessions – this is important in language classes;

- moving online offers the opportunity to guide students in more focussed self-study (especially in listening and reading practice);

- be aware that the online environment offers an immersive language experience of a different kind (increased emphasis on reading/writing, rather than oral/aural), and take measures to ensure content and processes are being understood appropriately;

- ensure scaffolding is in place to support students who are working at a distance and cannot physically ask questions/access support systems;

- utilise the staff, systems, and processes you have in a pragmatic way;

- work collaboratively and pull in support wherever you can find it; and

- respond to IT, and access issues as quickly as possible.

Although this article dwells mainly on technical matters, the experience gained in moving an entire PS course online at the fast pace dictated by the pandemic contributed to strengthening my belief in effective online education.

Prioritising pedagogy, learning design, and personal interaction and communication in online education are the roots to the successful facilitation of a transition from F2F to online language teaching and learning.

Acknowledgements

My thanks go to Nick Barratt, the Director of UoS PSs, and the hard-working and dedicated team of people who manage and teach in the UoS PS programme.

9 How to flip it... never again? Towards agile models of work

Marion Sadoux[1]

Abstract

This paper explores the way in which the Modern Languages team at the Oxford University Language Centre (OULC) sought to embrace the challenges of switching to a remote mode of teaching in the third term of 2019-20 as an opportunity to develop new ways of designing and delivering language courses for a flexible and hybrid future. It seeks to make note of agile recommendations towards further challenges to come.

Keywords: language teaching, delivery model, learning design, upskilling, elearning.

Back in January 2020, as I was preparing my presentation for the eLearning Symposium at the University of Southampton, I found myself contemplating the utterly disappointing use of eLearning to enhance the teaching and learning of languages in higher education, with an almost habitual sense of dread. I was reflecting on the all-too-familiar reduction of eLearning to its lowest possible common denominator – I use PPT – and on the difficulties I continued to encounter in my own career in convincing universities, let alone language teachers, that not all eLearning is bad or cheap, and that it can truly enhance teaching and learning. I had found an interesting survey in a recently published review of technology use in language teaching in higher education in the USA (Lomicka & Lord, 2019) the results of which were at once disappointing and unsurprising. They indicated that preferred practice (teachers and learners) remained strongly anchored to what one can best describe as face-to-face models

1. University of Oxford Language Centre, Oxford, United Kingdom; marion.sadoux@lang.ox.ac.uk; https://orcid.org/0000-0003-1875-6351

How to cite: Sadoux, M. (2021). How to flip it... never again? Towards agile models of work. In A. Plutino & E. Polisca (Eds), *Languages at work, competent multilinguals and the pedagogical challenges of COVID-19* (pp. 89-95). Research-publishing.net. https://doi.org/10.14705/rpnet.2021.49.1222

of delivery in which technology plays a very limited role. This resonated with my own experience in different institutions and with the resistance encountered in terms of shifting practices from an educational engineering perspective. This resistance, I must say, is often 'legitimate', as language teachers in higher education rarely have the status, the salary, the time, the encouragement, or the opportunities to develop the critical engagement that would be required to genuinely transform professional practice (or to truly professionalise that practice).

Then came COVID-19 and the great flip! All of a sudden, the tools of eLearning had to be deployed across the sector.

At Oxford University, in some ways, we were lucky. The OULC had been an early adopter of the new Virtual Learning Environment (VLE), Canvas, which was still in its early implementation phase; we had also been piloting our first fully online language courses in French, German, and Spanish, and the next phase of online courses were due to start in the run up to Easter. Use of the VLE to support face-to-face teaching was patchy though, and greatly varied among tutors and languages. With Canvas, we had a VLE which offered excellent affordances for languages, particularly with the seamless integration of video and voice tools – sadly, something that very few tutors had previously sought to use at all.

The switch to 'remote' teaching came later for us; our second term (Hilary term) was reaching its natural end as we made the decision to shut our doors on March 17th. We cancelled the face-to-face intensive courses that were due to start the week after the end of term; teachers and students, by then, had become very nervous. We then had a period of planned review meetings and staff development for the ensuing two weeks, followed by a long break leading to our third term of teaching, which started in late April. So, we flipped and met online – first in the virtual classroom provided by the open source web conferencing 'Big Blue Button', where we also held daily lunchtime social meetings in an effort to 'normalise' and 'humanise' the use of the synchronous video conferencing.

Unlike many others, we were able to observe, listen to, and see the difficulties encountered in the sector by those who had to pivot overnight to online delivery. Unlike most others, we also subsequently had an entire term to experiment with the remote teaching model that we had designed, collect feedback from our learners, and run a second iteration of courses as intensive online summer courses, whilst also tweaking the model of delivery. Another dimension that supported our endeavours was, without a doubt, linked to the very structure of the institution – the devolved nature of the collegiate university offered a blanket protection against central top-down diktats, and left a lot of room to manoeuvre to develop bespoke solutions in response to our needs, our learners' needs, and our tutors' needs. As early adopters of the new VLE, we were also able to rely on our robust relationships with the learning technologists, who also played a considerable role in ensuring that Information Technology (IT) services were able to work around bespoke solutions for us. We were also fortunate in that the university was eager to invest in making sure that the quality of the teaching and learning experience remained high, and to limit any potential reputational damage.

This investment took various forms. In the OULC, the senior management team decided to acknowledge that the continuation of teaching would be on a best-efforts basis. We lowered the fees for all our courses by 25%, and we gave our learners the option to opt out of our year-long courses, and, if they wished or needed to, we offered them the option to take their assessments earlier than scheduled. Some 67% of our learners in those year-long courses opted to continue, giving us a strong sense of trust.

Another form of investment came in the establishment within the OULC of a peer-mentoring scheme. The workshops and meetings held during the two-week lead up to the Easter vacation were critical in developing the structure of the delivery model and in further analysing and understanding the needs of the team in terms of upskilling and support. This helped craft a strong case for additional spending to buy time throughout the third term. The early online teaching practitioners who had collaborated to the development of our online course pilots became mentors. This scheme enabled us to have daily mentoring sessions with tutors who needed support and for general trouble shooting; this small group of mentors were also able to have weekly meetings in order to identify needs that could be met through a more generic and sustained intervention. Finally, a bespoke container (or course) on the VLE was set up to host all the required guidance, templates, video tutorials on how to use or set up certain tools, questions, discussions, and sharing of best practices. At the start of our remote teaching term, I had already spent over 100 hours setting up this platform, and, throughout the 11 weeks of the term, tutors spent an average of 58 hours each making use of its resources. The investment in time that our tutors dedicated to this transformation – painful for some, an epiphany for others – was exceptional in all the senses of the word, enormous and not to be taken as an acceptable norm!

What did we do exactly? We reconfigured what had thus far been an implied model of face-to-face delivery (in reality, covering wide ranging and disparate practices) to work for online teaching. Tutors were given a template to follow. I purposely directed the work away from what seemed a disastrous and ubiquitous model of a 100% switch to online synchronous replacement of face-to-face interactions, and, instead, designed a hybrid flexible template that would also have the potential to shape future practice in a more homogenous way. Most importantly, the hybrid mix of asynchronous and synchronous elements aimed to ensure maximal access and engagement from learners, irrespective of their access to good broadband. If our online course pilots had taught us one thing, it was indeed not to rely too much on the quality of sound in live sessions. In this model, represented in Figure 1 below, synchronous online sessions are short and designed exclusively for the purpose of learner spoken interactions that have been scaffolded by the asynchronous learning pathway; there, the tutor becomes a guide and a facilitator, but leaves the centre stage to the learners as much as possible.

The learning pathways follow a rigid template in terms of navigational layout and structure, including seemingly annoying details such as how long learners should expect to spend on a given section.

Figure 1. Model for designing and delivering language courses

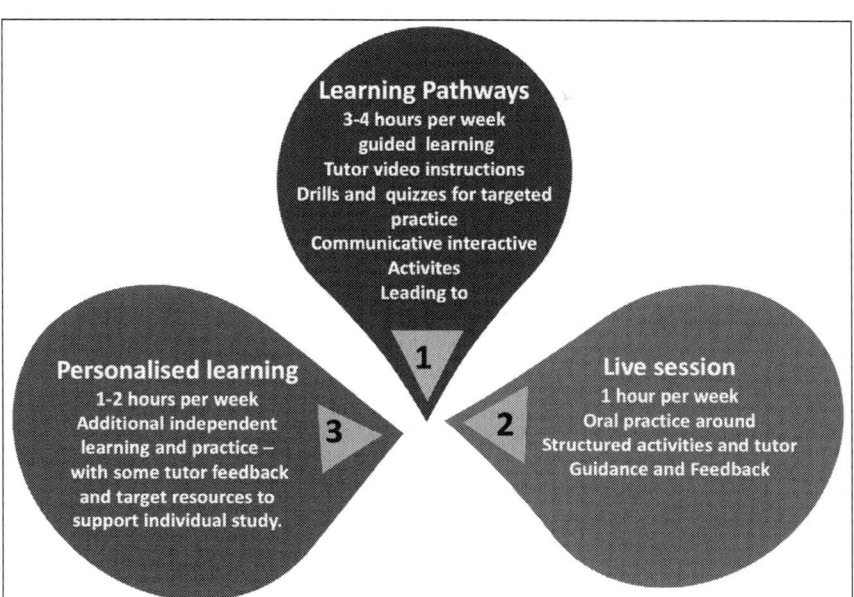

The way we worked had to change radically. From time spent with learners in a classroom, we shifted to time spent on the creation of learning pathways, the monitoring of discussions, and the production of feedback. This was resourced through a reduction in teaching load, and in the closing or postponed scheduling (as online intensives at the end of term) of some courses. Tutors had to spend less time on live delivery to be able to undertake the rest of the design work mentioned above.

This required intensive monitoring, feedback, support, and multiple check points to ensure that learners were satisfied and that tutors were coping. A small number of students felt that going from three hours of face-to-face teaching down to 30 minutes in class was not sufficient, and asked for the full three hours to be reinstated; some felt that they had had to work harder, and appreciated being able to distribute the time flexibly. The vast majority of the feedback, though, was positive, and a high number of learners commented on the superiority, in their view, of this delivery model. As one learner put it, "providing detailed/specific material to go through before the session helps to focus learning".

Looking back, what we accomplished – in disparate ways and in different styles, even within the structure of a template – is literally awesome. Many language teachers have had to learn a new way to do their job; faced with new daunting technology they would never have chosen to use, many have experienced moments of despair, ranging from frustration to alienation. We must pause for a moment and reflect on the tensions between what we gained and what we lost, what we committed in terms of good will, time, and effort, and what a realistic professional expectation going forward could be. Where do we go from now to make sure this never happens again? How do we learn the lesson of what lesson we need to learn?

Arguably, for the shifts in beliefs, attitudes, and identity, as well as the necessary new ways of working that we needed to develop, the role of our institutions locally and across the sector in easing or worsening such tensions is more critical than ever. We need fair instruments to account for the changes brought to our ways of working, and we need to make sure that, rather than responding to a single crisis (COVID-19), we are building resilience towards a sustainable future which we are able to embrace as it emerges. Developing this agility is not really about technology – it is about inventing new ways of collaborating, new ways of learning together, and constantly rethinking, recreating, and prototyping what we do.

We have an opportunity to re-evaluate what good teaching and learning is, and how to best respond to the needs of diverse learners in different institutions. We need to carefully rethink what this means in terms of skills, knowledge, and expertise from teachers and learners, and we need to ensure that, whilst we support the development of new competencies, we are equally sensitive to the problematic uprooting this may engender in relation to professional identity, core values, and beliefs. We need new tools to account for time needed in this adjustment. One essential thing that eLearning can provide us with is an ecology of learning which opens towards more agile and sustainable ways of working – together and in communities of practice.

Reference

Lomicka, L., & Lord, G. (2019). Reframing technology's role in language teaching: a retrospective report. *Annual Review of Applied Linguistics, 39*, 8-23. https://doi. org/10.1017/s0267190519000011

10 Moving the year abroad online: ready, steady, go!

Sonia Cunico[1]

Abstract

Exeter students who had their 2019-2020 Year Abroad (YA) cut short by the COVID-19 health crisis were offered alternative online language provision to support their learning. This contribution discusses the students and staff's experience in the light of 'learning is a journey' metaphor.

Keywords: year abroad, online teaching, learning metaphors.

COVID-19 has had a seismic effect on everybody and, although the cost in terms of human lives and economy will not be known for many years, its implications for teaching and learning are already palpable to everyone working in education. If there is a silver lining in the very dark COVID-19 sky, it is that the pandemic has accelerated a process which was already on the distant horizon. From January 2020 Modern Languages and Cultures at Exeter offered a YA online provision on Microsoft Teams to the students who had to return earlier than planned to the United Kingdom due to the COVID-19 health crisis. Even if limited in time and scope, and designed as a one-off experience, the provision was instrumental to help us navigate the stormy waters which engulfed us in the following months.

In this contribution I will build upon the metaphor of 'learning as a journey', which students undertake with the tutors and classmates, and discuss the feedback we received from students who took part in the YA online provision.

1. University of Exeter, Exeter, United Kingdom; s.cunico@exeter.ac.uk

How to cite: Cunico, S. (2021). Moving the year abroad online: ready, steady, go! In A. Plutino & E. Polisca (Eds), *Languages at work, competent multilinguals and the pedagogical challenges of COVID-19* (pp. 97-103). Research-publishing.net. https://doi.org/10.14705/rpnet.2021.49.1223

These reflections and considerations will help us shape our YA provision in the future and might be of inspiration to others.

The link between language and cognition, and hence the role of metaphors in communication and cognition, is well recognised in cognitive and linguistic research because the way in which language is used expresses, as well as reflects, creates, reinforces, or opposes, ways of making sense of aspects of our life and human experiences which are often difficult to express.

Metaphors We Live by Lakoff and Johnson (1980) offered a new cognitive conceptualisation of metaphors in which they are not simply linguistic embellishments used mainly in literature, but a way to make sense of complex and abstract human experiences through much more concrete ones to which we can more easily relate. From Ulysses to Dante, the 'journey' is a key metaphor for many of our experiences, and it also plays an important role in the way learners, as well as language teachers, talk about their own experience of teaching and learning a foreign language (Block, 1992; Ellis, 2001; Cortazzi & Jin, 1999).

The YA experience naturally lends itself to be expressed in terms of a material and psychological journey which thousands of students undertake each year. As I write, many students had to reconcile themselves with the fact that their YA plans have been disrupted since either travelling to their destination is impossible, or the experience is online.

Like any successful journey, the move online requires preparation and planning to ensure time is well spent and every aspect of the experience is considered and addressed. Teaching online leaves little room for improvisation: instructions must be shared beforehand, activities must be structured, well-paced and linked, and connections made all the time to ensure all participants are on board and able to follow the information given. The intensity of it is stressful and tiring; online synchronous teaching is highly performative for students, but above all for tutors who must map out the students' journey very carefully. The road map of the lessons must be shared with students who need to understand the direction of travel. This element comes out clearly from students' comments, with frequent references to 'structure':

> "It was very **clearly structured** and we knew what every session was going to be about and what to prepare" (R1).

> "Really **well thought out**, engaging classes with enthusiastic teachers" (R2).

Although it is clearly not possible to replace the YA experience with a virtual one, some steps were taken to ensure that the move online put students at the centre of it, offering them a strong experiential involvement crucial to the success of the project.

The virtual YA required, therefore, opportunities for cultural growth and expansion of one's cultural boundaries and understanding in ways which are meaningful and realistic, like a material journey. A virtual reality was explored and built upon the many resources made available online for free: museums were visited, cities were toured, and people met online.

Although the tutors were the tour operators who behind the scene were planning the journey, the emphasis was on students' involvement and co-participation. Working alone or in small groups, they had to complete three hours' preparation work before the Teams synchronous contact hour. The students were not just taken to a place; they had to get there by using the map of resources provided by the tutor. This commitment was an important aspect of the course to ensure deep learning and engagement with the resources and it was noted by students:

> "The sessions had quite a lot of preparation which was good because oral classes often need structure to sustain a conversation" (R7).

> "The tasks we were set involved watching films, documentaries, studying significant periods in the countries' history, learning about

music etc, and a lot of this I wouldn't have known about or looked into by myself" (R34).

The last comment (R34) highlights the role of the tutor/tour operator who guides the participants and takes them to places they would not have visited alone. The emphasis on a full immersion learning experience with virtual tours was at the core of some resources and activities which allowed students to move virtually to new places. Thus replicating (as much as possible) the real journey experience, to the point that for one student the boundaries between the real and virtual experience of living abroad became blurred:

> "I enjoyed the opportunity to learn about Spanish culture and **live in two beautiful cities** (Barcelona and Palma de Mallorca)" (R37).

For learners of a foreign language, one of the most pleasurable and important moments of our travels is meeting 'the locals' and engaging in social interactions through the foreign language. But how could we possibly recreate such encounters for students 'locked' in their bedroom or living at home with their parents? At Exeter we felt it was important not to miss out on the opportunity to engage on a daily basis with native speakers; in the case of Chinese, for example, we paired the Exeter home students who were forced to cut their YA short with our Chinese postgraduate students. Rather than being pre-packed with fixed and pre-designed syllabi and learning outcomes limiting students' agency, the sessions aimed to develop genuine communicative needs. Overall, students' feedback was positive especially because the contact was very intense (one hour per day) in order to ensure daily contact with native speakers:

> "We were given language partners with which to speak to for 5 hours per week, so me and my language partner would speak for one hour a day. **This was invaluable!!**" (R6).

However, the student's comment below also points to a mismatch of expectations which can lead to dissatisfaction:

"Using Masters students from China as a substitute for oral classes is not a good way to learn. Sometimes **they feel too embarrassed to correct all of our mistakes and are also not qualified teachers so aren't always able to verbalise what we have done incorrectly to help us learn from our mistakes**" (R22).

The aim of the matching was to increase fluency rather than accuracy, and it is important that in the future we (1) put in place some training for the native speakers (for instance, in error correction, etc.), but at the same time (2) ensure that their role is clarified to the YA students so expectations are managed.

The move online of the YA offers the opportunity to engage learners with real language use in meaningful social contexts, but this entails setting up innovative ways to put students in contact transnationally. In 2020-2021 Exeter students will be able to take advantage of EUniTa[2]: a dedicated and self-contained online platform accessible to any student from our EU Partner Institutions. Students will easily sign up for a tandem language exchange, get matched automatically, and find all the needed communication tools within the platform itself. This requires a reconfiguration of our understanding of where and how students engage with language learning in tandem language schemes, what linguistic and specific knowledge they can develop autonomously, and how their specific discipline interests and competence should be considered in a language tandem scheme to help students become part of a wider community of language learners.

One of the biggest challenges we face with online teaching is creating a sense of purposeful group identity in which learners feel safe and trust each other. As with real journeys, feeling comfortable with each other is key to the experience, but creating personal relationships online may be problematic due to the lack of opportunities for small talk and casual exchanges from which deeper ones can grow. Tutors, therefore, must ensure that preference is given to the design of small group work or one-to-one activities to allow personal relationships to develop within the ecosystem which is the language class. It is important to

2. https://www.eunita.org/

recognise that the virtual language classes are an important social occasion for many students who may rely on them to feel part of a reality outside the four walls of their bedrooms as the following comments exemplify:

"My class bonded so much and I really loved signing into our daily calls. When we are back in Exeter you will all receive some Finnish chocolate when the COVID-19 situation allows it!" (R15).

"The classes were very structured [...] we also had time to converse more informally which I think helped us all to relax in such a new type of teaching environment" (R17).

Preparation is key to the success of the journey, but after the overnight shift to online teaching and learning caused by the pandemic, this now requires massive investment by universities; not just in terms of Information Technology (IT) infrastructure, but also, and very importantly, pedagogical training to be set up quickly to facilitate staff's planning. The sector at large has also intervened to facilitate as smooth a transition as possible with a great spirit of collegiality. Since April 2020, both the University Council Modern Languages[3] and the Association of University Language Communities[4] have organised training sessions and also weekly open catch-up sessions for professionals to exchange, not just ideas and best practice, but also concerns and worries about the transition online (UCML, n.d.).

While we continue moving our teaching online, we may feel overwhelmed by the challenges that the transition requires. The international health crisis also calls for constant adjustments and quick changes of plans, and more than ever staff and tutors alike need to be resilient. To use another travelling metaphor, we are in uncharted waters. Like tour operators, tutors must map the journey and identify the learning goals and destinations; but also be ready to change route if needed, while keeping an eye on their travelling companions, the learners, to

---

3. https://university-council-modern-languages.org/

4. http://www.aulc.org/

ensure they are having a positive learning experience. More than ever before the teaching and learning process must embrace virtual realities which have become a common experience during the lockdown period, and which are now part of our new normal.

References

Block, D. (1992). Metaphors we teach and learn by. *Prospect, 7*(3), 42-55.

Cortazzi, M., & Jin, L. (1999). Bridges to learning: metaphors of teaching, learning and language. In L. Cameron & G. Low (Eds), *Researching and applying metaphor* (pp. 149-176). Cambridge University Press. https://doi.org/10.1017/cbo9781139524704.011

Ellis, R. (2001). The metaphorical constructions of second language learners. In M. Breen (Ed.), *Learner contribution to language learning: new directions in research*. Pearson Education.

Lakoff, G., & Johnson, M. (1980). *Metaphors we live by*. University of Chicago Press.

UCML. (n.d.). *Year abroad: supporting virtual mobility*. University Council Modern Languages. https://university-council-modern-languages.org/year-abroad/

11 Studying languages in the times of COVID-19: reflections on the delivery of teaching and learning activities and the year abroad

Sascha Stollhans[1]

Abstract

This contribution reflects on some of the challenges the COVID-19 pandemic has introduced for languages in Higher Education (HE). In particular, two areas are discussed: the delivery of teaching and learning activities, including assessments, and the year abroad. These two areas, on which the enforced move to online provision has had a significant impact, are central to many UK languages degrees. The piece discusses challenges, responses, and unresolved issues. All in all, it aims to offer a positive view for the future of the sector by highlighting particularly the spirit of collegiality that has developed during the pandemic across different HE institutions and national organisations.

Keywords: languages, COVID-19, year abroad, assessments, digital teaching, collaboration.

The COVID-19 pandemic has brought about a number of challenges that directly impact the educational landscape across all subjects. The languages sector offers a unique perspective on how the pandemic is affecting the approach to teaching and learning for subjects in which close student-tutor interaction and immersive elements are often deemed essential for successful learning and the attainment of learning objectives. The sudden move to online teaching and learning, to

1. Lancaster University, Lancaster, United Kingdom; s.stollhans@lancaster.ac.uk; https://orcid.org/0000-0002-9352-174X

How to cite: Stollhans, S. (2021). Studying languages in the times of COVID-19: reflections on the delivery of teaching and learning activities and the year abroad. In A. Plutino & E. Polisca (Eds), *Languages at work, competent multilinguals and the pedagogical challenges of COVID-19* (pp. 105-111). Research-publishing.net. https://doi.org/10.14705/rpnet.2021.49.1224

supplant conventional student-tutor interaction, has left little time to plan for such a transition with any amount of foresight. The mandatory period of isolation and the subsequent surge in digital practices may continue to have an impact on, and potentially influence, pedagogy in the post-pandemic world. However, it is not just classroom pedagogy that has been affected and requires modification. From admissions and recruitment to research dissemination – all areas in which a languages department operates – have been affected in some form, and in all areas staff and students have had to develop new skills or repurpose existing skills.

In this piece, I reflect on two areas that form central parts of languages degrees at many UK universities: the delivery of teaching and learning activities (including assessments), and the year abroad/the organisation of international placements. As both a teacher of German and an international placement year (year abroad) tutor in the Department of Languages and Cultures at Lancaster University, I have had first-hand experience of the developments in these two areas. In my reflections, I focus on some key challenges the sector has experienced and consider how we have approached these in our department and as a sector. Taking stock, I also aim to highlight some potential positive opportunities that have arisen, particularly relating to the acquisition and enhancement of skills for staff and students. Lastly, I will identify questions that remain unanswered at this point and need further, potentially sector-wide, discussions.

The delivery of teaching and learning activities is arguably the area in which departments have seen the most drastic changes caused by the pandemic. Sudden campus closures meant that classes had to move online, facilitated via Zoom, Microsoft Teams, or similar platforms. This has understandably led to concerns among both staff and students: will online classes be just as effective as face-to-face classes? How do they need to be adapted for the new environment to avoid unsuccessfully replicating face-to-face classes online?

While many, if not all, HE institutions are well versed in using online platforms and digital tools to supplement their teaching, most are not usually equipped for, and experienced in, delivering their portfolios entirely online (The Open

University being a notable exception). For both staff and students, this has meant a period of having to familiarise themselves with new online platforms, experimenting with software and different approaches, and, no doubt, some degree of overload and frustration.

In preparation for the academic year 2020/2021, Lancaster University has, for the majority of its teaching and learning activities, moved to blended learning models; combining synchronous online sessions with asynchronous elements, such as recorded video tutorials, preparatory exercises, and tutor-facilitated online discussions.

Preparing for this blended learning model has also been an opportunity for staff to re-visit and draw on previous experiences with digital practice. For instance, I had been working on the use of audio-visual screencast tools for a number of years, exploring its impact on student engagement with feedback (Speicher & Stollhans, 2015) but also more recently looking at ways in which screencast feedback can improve linguistic accuracy and complexity of academic texts produced by students. While this is not an approach I discovered and started exploring due to the pandemic, and the subsequent enforced move to online teaching and assessments, my previous experience with it has helped me re-think assessments during this time. I worked closely with one of our digital learning facilitators to further explore and share how the work I had previously done in this area could be usefully applied to the new context (Hosseini & Stollhans, 2020).

These forms of collaboration are a highly important and positive development: there has been an emergence of online initiatives that enable practitioners to share experiences, good practice, materials, but also concerns and anxieties. For the first time ever, the annual Innovative Language Teaching and Learning at University Conference (InnoConf)[2], and the annual conference of the European Association for Computer-Assisted Language Learning (EuroCALL)[3], took

---

2. https://conferences.ncl.ac.uk/innoconf20/

3. http://www.eurocall-languages.org/

place online in 2020, along with many other conferences and seminars such as the Kent Modern Languages Teaching Forum[4]. The Association for German Studies (AGS)[5] in Great Britain and Ireland postponed their annual conference, but put on a series of timely online events, including a social gathering.

In the same spirit, the Association of University Language Communities (AULC)[6] in the UK and Ireland has been holding weekly informal drop-in sessions on Microsoft Teams to provide a platform where colleagues can share and discuss both concerns and examples of good practice. Organisations such as the University Council of Modern Languages (UCML)[7] and the Institute of Modern Languages Research (IMLR)[8] were quick to collate a varied range of online materials, and create rich open-access repositories with the intention of supporting languages research and teaching. All these initiatives provide not only useful resources and opportunities, but they are also testament to the immensely collaborative and collegial spirit within the sector.

Examinations and assessments are an area that has shown to pose particular challenges. If traditional 'physical' written and oral examinations and tests cannot be conducted, what are the alternatives? At Lancaster University, the majority of examinations were cancelled and replaced with coursework assessments in the form of online tests on Moodle and take-home papers. With the aim of putting together an overview of practices at different institutions, we have conducted an online survey and shared this within the sector (Polisca, Stollhans, Bardot, & Rollet, forthcoming). The results, based on responses from colleagues at 24 different institutions, indicate that there has been no unified approach to the modification of assessments; rather, a variety of different solutions has been found, which included cancelling or replacing certain elements of assessment packages. An area of particular concern (raised by practitioners

4. https://research.kent.ac.uk/languages-teaching-forum/, see https://www.youtube.com/watch?v=RM9bDB-5y_8 for a recording of this year's online event

5. http://www.ags.ac.uk/2020online

6. http://www.aulc.org/

7. https://university-council-modern-languages.org/languages-education/online-resource-sharing/

8. https://modernlanguages.sas.ac.uk/about-us/online-resources

from 19 institutions in the survey) is how the changed circumstances have been affecting practices and existing guidelines concerning academic integrity and plagiarism. In this respect, different ad-hoc solutions have been trialled, but a sophisticated consistent approach remains to be found and implemented.

The year abroad, which is mandatory for students taking a languages degree at many UK universities, is often seen as a pivotal part of the degree. It offers an opportunity for students to immerse themselves in the language(s) and culture(s) they are studying, and to develop a range of intercultural and transferable skills. It has therefore been argued to have a positive impact on employability, and students often consider it to be a simultaneously daunting and rewarding experience (c.f. Salin, Hall, & Hampton, 2018 for a collection of insightful papers on all these aspects).

For the year abroad, COVID-19 has not only introduced concerns related to students' health, safety, and wellbeing, but also tangible organisational and legal issues that surpass the remit and expertise of year abroad tutors: what happens if the Foreign and Commonwealth Office recommends against any but essential travel to the country a student is planning to complete a placement in? – and is the year abroad, as a compulsory component of a university degree, considered to be 'essential' in this respect? What are the implications for health and travel insurance? If a student cannot travel abroad, what are the alternatives? How do we ensure students still meet the defined learning outcomes to a sufficient degree and still develop the range of linguistic, intercultural, and professional skills a placement abroad would have offered them?

At this point in time, many of these questions remain unanswered. The uncertainty and fluidity of the situation, combined with student expectations and, quite understandably, anxieties, has put significant pressures on year abroad tutors and coordinators, international offices, and heads of departments. The UCML has set up a Special Interest Group *Year abroad: supporting virtual mobility* "with a view to mitigating the impact [the pandemic] will have on Modern Languages undergraduates due to undertake a Year Abroad in the academic year 2020-2021" (UCML, 2020, p. 1). The group, of which 47 universities are members, has set out four principles: to send students abroad if and when this is possible, while applying flexibility with respect to required placement periods; to continue to welcome exchange students from partner universities ('physically' or online); to create and share a range of virtual activities; to encourage individual institutions to apply flexibility; and offer alternatives to their year abroad assessment formats and requirements.

While online placements are a valuable experience in themselves and offer the opportunity to develop linguistic, professional, digital, and transferable skills, they are unlikely to provide the same immersive and culturally rich experience as the year abroad. A combination of virtual and 'physical' placements (whenever these are possible and safe) may have to be the way forward for the academic year 2020/2021 and most immediate future. In any case, the year abroad will be an even more individual and personalised undertaking, and year abroad tutors will need to work closely with students to discuss individual circumstances and explore different options specific to each student.

As I finish writing these reflections, we are still in the middle of the pandemic. Whatever happens, one thing seems clear: staff and students have shown a considerable amount of flexibility, adaptability, and optimistic productivity. On many occasions digital skills have been enhanced, adapted, and newly developed, and creative new approaches have been found to make the best of a difficult situation.

There are problems that we have yet to find solutions for, such as in the area of teaching and learning delivery. Plagiarism and academic malpractice frameworks for digital assessments also need to be developed, trialled, and implemented. To make a success of the year abroad during the pandemic, we will need to find ways to offer opportunities for linguistic and cultural immersion in the absence of, or hopefully rather in addition to, in-situ placements. Virtual exchange programmes and virtual reality immersion may offer potential solutions.

One common thread that runs through all the observations I have shared in this piece concerns the way in which the sector has been working together more closely than ever. It is inspiring how colleagues have been supporting each other across institutional and geographical borders, and how many initiatives have been informed by joined-up thinking and cross-institutional collaborations.

References

Hosseini, D., & Stollhans, S. (2020). *Podcast "Digital Education Practices: What works?", Episode 5: Personal connections: how audiovisual feedback increases students' understanding.* https://digitaleducationpractices.com/2020/05/11/episode-4-personal-connections-how-audiovisual-feedback-increases-students-understanding-2/

Polisca, E., Stollhans, S., Bardot, R., & Rollet, C. (forthcoming). How Covid-19 has changed language assessments in higher education: a practitioners' view.

Salin, S., Hall, D., & Hampton, C. (2018). (Eds). Perspectives on the year abroad: a selection of papers from YAC2018. Research-publishing.net. https://doi.org/10.14705/rpnet.2020.39.9782490057573

Speicher, O., & Stollhans, S. (2015). Feedback on feedback – does it work? In F. Helm, L. Bradley, M. Guarda & S. Thouësny (Eds), *Critical CALL – proceedings of the 2015 EUROCALL Conference, Padova, Italy* (pp. 507-511). Research-publishing.net. https://doi.org/10.14705/rpnet.2015.000384

UCML. (2020). *Virtual mobility principles.* University Council of Modern Languages. https://university-council-modern-languages.org/wp-content/uploads/2020/06/UCML-Virtual-Mobility-Statement.pdf

12 Exploring the pandemic through language learning and multicultural studies

Stephan Caspar[1]

Abstract

This piece offers a reflection on how language learning and multicultural studies during the pandemic have highlighted the potential to help communities draw parallels with, and face wider issues concerning, minorities within a challenged society. Through storytelling, a novel approach to teaching and learning helps students find their voice and become active agents of change. A review of teaching and learning methods may bring about improvements both in academia and individual circumstances to help bridge the gap between loneliness and the need to be part of a wider social community. This article reiterates the importance of language learning, cultural understanding, and identity as useful employability skills for the new global graduates to support, rebuild, and unite communities especially in challenging times.

Keywords: multilingualism, learner communities, LGBTQi+, Black lives.

In the months since lockdown, as the world reacted to a global pandemic, educators have been forced to explore ways to continue teaching. In the move to *remote learning,* we have needed to adapt and redesign learning for a new setting, somewhere between an online course and a classroom. Unable to carry out face-to-face instruction we have asked ourselves what this space is, what is *emergency remote learning*?

1. Carnegie Mellon University, Pittsburgh, Pennsylvania, United States; scaspar@andrew.cmu.edu; https://orcid.org/0000-0002-3512-4228

How to cite: Caspar, S. (2021). Exploring the pandemic through language learning and multicultural studies. In A. Plutino & E. Polisca (Eds), *Languages at work, competent multilinguals and the pedagogical challenges of COVID-19* (pp. 113-118). Research-publishing.net. https://doi.org/10.14705/rpnet.2021.49.1225

As a British academic currently working at a US university, the political and social tensions that have surfaced during the pandemic have forced me to rethink my teaching and examine the support that I provide for students, for whom the upheaval has been nothing short of traumatic. Many have struggled to adapt, are understandably anxious about their futures, and, forced to spend time in front of screens writing, reading, and watching, they question the cost of their education.

The courses I teach in language learning and multicultural studies aim to provide students with the tools to tell stories about their own experiences, exploring how culture and language have shaped their identity. Many students find it challenging to be asked to express themselves in this way and shape outcomes that are uniquely personal. While there are no 'right' answers to many of the topics we discuss, frameworks and theories guide us through moral and philosophical complexities to help us better understand our context. Through digital storytelling, students produce outcomes that speak to these reflections and mirror aspects of their own relationship with culture and language.

The students I meet are with rare exception multilingual, mostly bilingual, and many competent with a third or even fourth language. They are international students and American students, Black students and students of Colour drawing on a life lived in heritage communities as Asian American, Indian American, African American, Hispanic and Latino, Arab Americans, and the interwoven identities of their families and neighbourhoods. They live at the intersection of language, moving between lingua Franca, patios, creole, local dialects, slang; mixing words, and blending conversations to suit the context, generation, setting, and amplifying meaning.

When the world changed and coronavirus spread into our lives some students returned home, some remained in halls or shared houses, some were still abroad or travelling. All seemed to want to somehow keep learning, so we moved online and taught remotely. I built an office in the sunroom on the side of our house and hastily assembled media and recording equipment and made space to teach.

The faces on the screen, those students whom I had taught in class, initially looked slightly dazed and unsure. I tried to express empathy and provide some reassurance as they adjusted to their circumstances. Some students returned home, learning how to live as families again after time apart, they shared meals and stories; many helped to support the household, working on the front lines in supermarkets, chemists, as delivery drivers, and some handing out food packages or helping elderly neighbours. They tried to stay active, grateful for flexibility, and understanding from their teachers and instructors as they adjusted to the changes in their lives. It seemed as if everyone was *making do*, coping with being back home in sometimes challenging conditions, sharing rooms with siblings, contributing to the household; many sharing feelings of loneliness and anxiety about coping during this time.

I thought that I might be more prepared than others as an experienced learning technologist with an understanding of online learning and familiarity with tools and apps. Eager to share and support, I wrote a quick piece about transition, just as I was organising myself. I talked about the online space, the value of online facilitation, and the distinction between synchronous and asynchronous learning. I was grateful for other voices too; those reminding us of the pressures faced by students, that this wasn't online learning, but something else, *emergency remote instruction*. This reminder was useful and helped me shape my strategy for the coming months. Firstly, I stripped the curriculum of everything that was deemed superfluous, additional, or extra work. I refocused on the core learning aims and reduced expected workload. I also looked at ways to make things fun and light, to ensure active learning would take place in this online space in which students would actively participate and not just passively listen.

The course looked better as a result. I settled on a weekly routine of synchronous and asynchronous activity. Starting on a Monday morning with a short announcement for the week, I laid out the aims and sign-posted learning steps built in our learning management system (Canvas). We established a backchannel, using Slack as a space to discuss ideas, share content, and answer questions. On Thursdays we met as a class using Zoom, and the sessions would include discussion and breakout rooms where catching up and sharing news was as crucial as addressing a prompt. We tried different tools, enjoyed demos, guest speakers (I thank the generosity of all those who put themselves forward), and played games. We dressed up, introduced mascots, attempted experiments, and challenged ourselves with quizzes. There seemed to be an almost optimistic sense, huddled inside with learning to shield ourselves from the danger outside. However, as just one class in a busy schedule, reports that other classes were still piling on the pressure, that students were being shamed for non-attendance or not turning the camera on, that some lecturers were doubling down on assignments and readings, became a depressingly familiar landscape. "Just get them through" became my mantra.

As we moved through the semester and summer, the initial novelty of remote learning wore off and the desire to return to the classroom became more keenly felt. We all missed the social contact, the purposeful rhythms of campus life, the institutional focus that is difficult to replicate online. We were adrift, at home.

In July, following the killings of George Floyd, Brianna Taylor, and Ahmaud Arbery, courageous protesters took to the streets to voice their anger at police brutality and centuries of systemic racism. We quickly realised the parallels, that racism is a pandemic, the murder of Black people. The protesters called against the suppression of Black voices, a system built to deny access to education, basic health care, and worker rights. This crisis, this disease of white supremacism that had killed for hundreds of years.

As multilinguals, heritage speakers, and international students and staff, events in the US made us reflect on racism in other countries, and the way civil unrest and protest are handled. We reflected in class on systems of oppression, discussing events across the world. We talked about language, the use of semantics, and the framing of events by politicians, the media, and those in power even in our own institutions.

Across the world, within Academia and Education, anger, sadness, and a desire for change expressed itself through articles and petitions, marches, and learn-ins. It was clear to many that more needed to be done; that as educators, humanists, and scholars we had a responsibility, not just to denounce racism and show solidarity, but be actively anti-racist and make changes in our own lives. It is to my shame that this came as a jolt, as I reflected on my own circumstance and privilege, as I thought about the ways that I could provide support and allyship at this time.

I looked more closely at my teaching, thinking about what I needed to re-address and educate myself by reading and listening. I resolved to better get to know my students, their histories and cultures; to amplify the voices and work of Black people and people of Colour in my teaching and recognise the intersectionality of Black LGBTQi+[2] lives. In my courses, I have always wanted to empower students as agents of change and to explore what that could mean as I reflected on who and what education is for.

Returning to first principles around education, I collected some of my favourite readings, from John Dewey to Paulo Freire, and introduced myself to Bell Hooks and Peter McLaren – educators and practitioners to inform my personal philosophy of education. I affirmed my own desire to teach using constructivist and experiential frameworks. I have never felt surer that my role is to provide a space to nurture caring and creative pedagogies, where students can express themselves, use language, and explore identity with freedom and without fear.

I taught throughout the summer, unable to attend conferences or travel; I made myself useful, wrote, and shared my experiences with others. As we enter a new semester, similar but different pressures exist, the world weary of pandemic and filled with uncertainty, facing decisions about reopening classrooms and resuming activities. Many of my peers are anxious and eager to return, especially those who have struggled with technology and see the socially distanced classroom as an imperfect improvement.

We are working and living through times of unrest and uncertainty and as educators we want to provide meaning, we want to create spaces where understanding can

---

2. Lesbian, gay, bisexual, transgender, queer, intersex, …

be formed. These times are taking their toll; as we reel from the human cost, the tragedy of over a million global deaths and more than 38 million people infected worldwide – as I am writing this article – the pandemic defines everything we do and will continue to shape our futures.

As educators, we have a role in shaping the futures of our students. We know that so many people are anxious about their future, but perhaps this is a moment to recognise and understand how learning about language, culture, and identity can help us support, rebuild, and unite communities. Systemic racism can only be dismantled by understanding our role within it. We can teach students to tell stories, amplify Black and Brown voices, and those marginalised and suppressed within our communities. Students can be agents of social change and build new futures. For our students, the hope is that the experience of having lived through a pandemic and through the Black Lives Matter protests may bring about resilience and empathy.

We must, however, continue to share perspectives and experiences. Multilingual perspectives can help shape discourse, and we can, and must, use language to tell stories and provide meaning. In the courses that I teach, I ask students to draw on their own cultural context to speak of others. We know that one way we can come together to address inequality and support each other is through learning. We have what it takes and that is each other.

Author index

Printed in Great Britain
by Amazon

60214746R00078